Also by Teresa Mateus

(formerly writing as Teresa B. Pasquale)

Mending Broken: A Personal Journey Through the Stages of Trauma and Recovery (2012)

Sacred Wounds: A Path to Healing from Spiritual Trauma (2015)

Mystic Soul Press
Chicago, IL, 60626
www.mysticsoulpress.com

ISBN Print: 978-1-7332788-0-5

ISBN E-Book: 978-1-7332788-1-2

FIRST EDITION

This book is a work of creative nonfiction and as such names have sometimes been changed or characters synthesized (from a number of people into one) for the purposes of storytelling.

Cover design by Teresa Mateus
Book design by Indie Publishing Group
Printed in the United States of America

Going Naked

THE CAMINO DE SANTIAGO & LIFE AS PILGRIMAGE

by Teresa Mateus

TO EVERYONE WHO HAS FALLEN DOWN AND LEARNED TO GET UP AND WALK AGAIN. TO SURVIVORS. TO THRIVERS. TO DREAMERS. TO TRAVELERS. AND TO THOSE WHO I AM BLESSED TO CALL FAMILY AND THE PLACES I HAVE FOUND HOME…SPIRITUALLY, MYSTICALLY, AND EMBODIED.

Contents

Barbara Holmes

PILGRIMAGE BEGINS WHEN we are born. We enter an ongoing stream of human existence and a lifelong spiritual journey. This is by necessity a faith walk, for we don't know where we are going, and we don't know when we will hit a bump in the road. All we know for certain is that "in this world we will have trouble." Teresa Mateus is in the midst of a life crisis when she begins her walk of faith on El Camino de Santiago. As Rabbi Abraham Joshua Heschel notes, the faith referenced "is not the clinging to a shrine, but an endless pilgrimage of the heart."

As it is with all of us, Mateus begins her pilgrimage long before she reaches El Camino. Her journey and ours is toward purpose, healing and transformation. Pilgrimage is also a momentary turning away from everyday life that allows us to participate in spiritual seeking. Theologian and author Eugene Peterson is quoted as saying, "The life of faith isn't meant for tourists. It's meant for pilgrims." But it takes courage to step off of life's merry-go-round to allow the divine's best intentions for us to manifest.

Like most pilgrims on a journey, Teresa is inevitably confronted with a body that won't always co-operate, a mind that will not stop its senseless chatter, and repressed wounds that surface during the silence of dark and starlit skies. But she is not stymied by any of this, as she deftly guides the reader through intersecting stories of her lifelong search for identity and rootedness. It is her story, but it is also ours. For our personal life paths do not always lead toward our highest hopes and dreams. Sometimes, our choices lead us toward tears and broken hearts, and sometimes trouble is not about us at all. It is cosmic preparation for the arc of leadership.

Mateus chronicles the necessity of surrender as an integral part of pilgrimage. She describes a flood of tears on a plane ride in a middle seat, between two family members, who seem not to notice or care about her distress. It continues with lost bags, the end of a marriage, and the reluctant but necessary letting go of emotional and spiritual baggage, and dreams that stand in the way of purpose.

The letting go is practical. We can carry all of our pain, disappointments and pride if we want to, but clutching our resentments may make it impossible to heal from the past and discern the future. We are on a journey toward our purpose, our healing and our transformation. This is not an easy endeavor. The seeking becomes even more difficult in the West because we are besieged with delusions of success, power, and wealth that masquerade as purpose.

Our delusions are so familiar and so tightly woven that we hardly ever know that we have created a "reality" that is not anchored to anything. Making stuff up is a collective enterprise that may be the only thing that western societies do well together. The very essence of healing is the willingness to move steadily away from the mirage of perpetual happy endings toward the rocky and sometimes uneven road toward transformation.

Although pilgrimages seem to be aimed toward specific geo-spiritual locations, they are actually oriented toward forgotten and hidden inner trails. Mateus is reuniting with her spiritual mother and patron, St Teresa of Ávila. But more importantly, she is being offered the opportunity to go naked through grief and pain toward her inner strength. From the first page to the last, she accepts this offer with deep listening and vulnerability. Through the power of her story, the reader is also invited to move toward their own metaphysical journeys that will be wondrous, difficult and transforming.

In *Going Naked*, Teresa journeys past one obstacle after another then offers practices at the end of each chapter that invite us to embark on a pilgrimage of the heart. I am grateful for her unveiling of her innermost struggles, so that we can continue to interrogate our own.

Origin Stories

MOTHERLESS CHILDREN & CHILDLESS MOTHERS

I WAS BORN on October 15, 1979. I don't begin here because it gives away how old I am or how many gray hairs are forlornly popping up on my dark brown head of hair these days (insert deep sigh), but rather because it alludes to a valuable part of my own origin story. One that shaped my life and my pilgrimage—as if those aren't inherently the same thing—in a very particular way. I was born on October 15, 1979 in Bogotá, Colombia. A country of the Andes Mountains, myths of gold, and where every part of my person was marinated in its lineage. I am brown. I am indigenous. I am Latinx. All of this was given birth to here—although much of it has taken a lifetime to birth out of its own dormancy, but that we will get to later. It is the country where I was first abandoned and first nurtured by mothers. It is amazing how much my origin story is saturated with a deep loss of mothering and a great abundance of it—and how it offered a pattern of motherhood that would fill my life's journey.

I was born to a woman named Alicia Mateus who was twenty-three years old when she gave me up for adoption to an orphanage named the Fundación para la Adopción de los Niños Abandonada or FANA in Bogotá. I say I was born in Bogotá, but the truth is, I can only know as far back as my origin story goes—to the orphanage itself. Maybe my birth mother traveled from a country town outside the city. I can't be sure. But Bogotá is the origin that I know. The certainty of my origin, beyond place, lies in my birthdate and the significance it has held throughout my lifeline leading back to the story of my naming. The orphanage, at the time, was run by the Grey Order of nuns which I have discovered was an order founded in Montreal, Canada—also in October. They had arrived at FANA in 1979, the year of my birth, to support the work of the foundress Señora Mercedes Rosario de Martinez at the request of a local priest, originally from Montreal, who had been living in Colombia for the previous fifteen years. So, there we were—me and the sisters—beginning a lifelong theme of nuns in my life.

Traditionally, the naming process of new babies to the orphanage was quite Dickensian (if anyone remembers how it all went down in *Oliver Twist*) where each baby was named based on the next letter of the alphabet—keeping that whole naming process tidy and uncomplicated. However, the nuns abdicated the process for me due to my birthdate. October 15th is the Catholic feast day of Teresa of Ávila, the fiery sainted nun from the hillsides of Spain, and as a result the sisters couldn't help but name me after her—and so I became Teresa for a first time. I also became Teresa Mateus for the first time.

I spent the next few months of life raised in the orphanage—one of many in a roomful of babies in an orphanage trying to meet the needs of an overabundance of abandoned children who formerly had no place to go when left by their birth parents. I would later realize how beautiful and painful this synchronicity of beginnings would be, and how much it would shape so much of my life, my story, my seeking and my subsequent journeying. I was a motherless child, raised by a community of childless mothers, and named by them after the sainted childless mother who would become the mother I was always seeking. Childless mothers and motherless children—this theme at the core of my origin has both devastated and filled my heart throughout my life.

A story of life that begins with abandonment is one that makes it hard to see through the fog of that pain into the abundance of love that is often just beyond its surface. It took me a good portion of my lifetime to see that a life born of motherlessness actually offered me an origin story of much more than that—it actually offered me an abundance of mothers.

Often, for orphanage children from marginalized lands, you are most likely to be adopted by parents from "first world" countries like England, Australia, the United States and changing your name from the one that you were given to something else more Anglo is the first customary erasure of origin. Prospective parents will come with their own list of names, based on their own family, histories and location. In this simple way erasure of origin happens, as a Latinx and Spanish name like Teresa gets changed to something white-presenting like Cindy, Martha or Jane. Interestingly, with the aid of my many mothers (plentiful and some timeless), this pattern was changed within my story.

When my adoptive parents arrived from Summit, New Jersey to Bogotá in February of 1980, they were greeted by the Grey Nuns and told the story of my naming. My adoptive mother, Patricia, told the sisters her own story. Her and my adoptive father, Michael, devout Catholics, had been trying to conceive a child for six years. During that time, they had endured multiple miscarriages and then the drawn-out process of international adoption. All the while they had been praying, in their church in Summit, for a child. Their church, they said with shared incredulity of synchronicity, was St. Teresa of Ávila Catholic Church. As a result, Teresa was one of the three names on their list of baby names they had brought from New Jersey. It seemed that by unanimous human and divine collective decision-making I was to be named Teresa, again.

In this way I was also connected in some root place, some origin moment, to Teresa of Ávila—a childless mother, giving birth to a motherless child, across time and all possibility. Alicia Mateus, my mother by birth, gave me the last name that I use now. A community of childless mothers and my adoptive mother doubly gave me my first name and in doing so not just rooted me to Teresa but a lineage of ancestry—Hispanic and Latinx, Colombian and Spanish. In the midst of it all, and through it all, Teresa of Ávila gave me the life that I live in so many ways. A life that also led me to the hillsides of Spain, to the Camino de Santiago, and on a pilgrimage, which for me, would close not at the end of the Camino but in the footsteps of my *other* birth mother—into Ávila, Spain.

BEYOND COMFORTABLY NUMB

Joseph Campbell, author of *The Power of Myth* and symbiotically known with the term "The Hero's Journey" was someone I stumbled upon at a particular rupture point in my life. I remember sitting on the couch in my townhouse in Fort Collins, Colorado. It was 2002 and I was twenty-two. I had just gotten out of a three-year relationship, full of dysfunction and dependency born of my own static PTSD from sexual trauma. The apartment had been gutted of our shared life, he had taken our dog when he left, and I was trying to figure out my next step. I knew I had to face the pain of my trauma to move forward but I didn't know where to begin. I was flicking through channels and landed on PBS, drawn in by this series called "The Power of Myth." Here I found Joseph Campbell and through him found the metaphor hidden in my own life, the parallels between life's path and the myth, the history and narratives of all lives throughout time. Finally, I discovered the way in which we are living out our own hero's journey through our hard places and into transformation—if we accept the invitation to transformation. It, by no means, made the path out of that particular dark night clear, but it made me see the meaning in and through and beyond myself in walking through it and finding my way to something more profound and beautiful. I wasn't walking it alone. I was walking it with a timeless army of pilgrims—who came before and after my own small life. We may be walking our own pilgrimage in our own lives alone—but we are not alone. We are deeply connected and profoundly intertwined.

Much of life offers us the off-ramp from transformation which I call being "comfortably numb." Comfortable numbness is the act of becoming comfortable even in our complacent and static places. These can even be painful places which, when held for long enough—bad or good, painful or bland, harmful or dysfunctional, becomes comfortable. Comfort is the antithesis of transformation. Which can also be ok. We don't always need to be in a state of transformation. That would be immensely exhausting. But without periodic transformation we become comfortably numb in our lives. When that happens, we often end up in places that are comfortable but aren't necessarily joyful or growth-oriented. This comfortable numbness can become encased in habits which help us avoid whatever we might need to be alive and aware, causing us to ignore our pain or not see the calling that is beckoning us forward. These habits can be things we see as benign or socially acceptable like shopping or gaming, occasional overeating or binge-watching television, or they can move into the realm of more overtly risky behaviors leading to addictions like alcohol and drugs, extensive gambling or compulsive sex.

For the years when I was married and living in Florida, I did work in addiction treatment. Southeast Florida had become the mecca of addiction recovery in the nation (fun fact if you didn't know) and I used Joseph Campbell's work extensively, and most specifically a beautiful retrospective documentary on his work and life called "Finding Joe." One of the things I would always tell folks in recovery is that there is a blessing in your suffering—your addictions are so obvious they force you to move into the pain and begin a transformational journey that so many others would avoid if given a choice.

Much of the world sits in a space of comfortable numbness, self-medicating in more subtle or socially acceptable ways, equally unhappy and unfulfilled, but without the impetus of deep breaking that often is required in order for us to transform.

This is so true. No truer and more visible than on the Camino's path, where so many people were working and walking through their hurt places to find some way out. We often have to have deep pain or deep life disruption, earthquake seismic shifts, to shake us out of our comfortable numbness. If I look back on the journeys of my life and the series of pilgrimages that changed the landscape of my experience, these were all born of a place of deep suffering and unavoidable seismic pain. The beauty of a pilgrim's journey is wherever we are we can always choose the on-ramp. We just have to be willing to do the work to move through the pain, let go of what isn't serving us, and embrace the change that comes from seeing into our own truth. As we do this the story of our own life becomes more visibly connected to the journeys before and after us, and more connected to the rest of our own lives. This is why origin stories can be so valuable. They allow us to see where we came from, what shaped our beginnings, and often offer up valuable information for the journey ahead.

In my research around terms, histories and lineages—which I love to immerse in as I begin to work on a new book or any new project—I uncovered an interesting synchronicity in my own origin story as it relates to the mythology of life unfolding. So often we the myth of our own journey in the cracks and broken places. We find it in the moments of synchronicity that show up unexpectedly. We find it when we are looking deeper into the invisible places. We find it when we dive into our pain and embrace our fear. We find it at the core of ourselves where it meets the core places of the world, of our collective histories, our myths and our beliefs.

I found a little hidden beauty as I dove into my own origin story. FANA (my orphanage), my origin place, my naming place, my only known birthplace, is also a word in Arabic—*fana*. It is a Sufi term meaning "passing away" or "annihilation" (of the self)—it means to die before dying. Fana is the depiction of the calling of pilgrimage. It is the pilgrimage. It calls us to be undone in order to be reborn.

My birthplace, when I sought the synchronicity at the root of it, also became the calling to me to be reborn through pilgrimage. Something in that can only be the symbiosis born of mythology, mystery and mystical truth. It is the root of the root. Pilgrimage is always beckoning us forward—down dusty trails, through painful travails, always calling us to become, again.

THE PRACTICE: Origin Story Mapping

The practice for the introduction asks you to remember your own origin story. This doesn't have to be your birth story, but it can be. It doesn't have to hit some specific marker in time but it's more important that it hits some deep part of yourself. What is your origin place or places. This can be one story or many.

Give yourself some time to consider what and who has shaped who you are, how you live life, what your meaning-making of your world is and where it came from. You can write about your ancestors, the people that came before you—known or unknown to you. You can write it as fantasy or mythology, as history or genealogy, as short story or poem, in a picture or a video. Use whatever way of expressing "where do I come from, who do I come from" that is meaningful to you.

Once you have done that, read and re-read or watch-rewatch it in a few sittings. See what comes up for you—what themes stick out, what elements bring up strong emotions and what are those emotions?

Take some time to write or draw, or video record some form of journaling about what you are noticing. This sets up the template of understanding your story of your life, your journeys, what has been and what will come. When we can see what shaped us—what is painful and beautiful—we can see how that informs our life and begin to consider how it created patterns that led to our comfortable numbness or transformation. The ingredients for both often lie in our origin stories.

Hold onto this material to refer back to throughout the process of this book and your movement through your own current journey of life.

Returning back to patterns and themes formed here and exhibited later in our own stories can be helpful to see how we have been shaped, what gives us strength and what takes that strength away.

CHAPTER 1

Fog & A Clearing

ON CAMINO: QUE SIMPLE

I THOUGHT PREPARATION was going to be the hard part of Camino. The planning, the packing, the finding of walking sticks and hiking boots equal to the task of a week of walking seemed like the most complicated elements of the trip from my home at the time in Boynton Beach, Florida to Santiago de Compostela, Spain. Silly, silly Teresa.

Getting to Santiago on time was already a bust. I was detoured and delayed by a one-day unplanned stopover in Barcelona. Already behind. My poor friend Marisol and her father had been waiting to pick me up at the airport in Santiago the morning of our planned beginning, and when I found out my flight wouldn't be arriving for another day they turned around and headed back to their family house in the hills above Santiago de Compostela. Marisol's family was part Honduran, on her mom's side, and part Galician (the regional identity of people from the area of Spain in and surrounding Santiago) on her father's side. They had a family house in the hills outside of Santiago and the plan had been to meet up at Santiago airport and then get a ride from Marisol's father to Sarria, the starting point of our 100-kilometer trek back towards Santiago.

Marisol and my friendship had flourished during graduate school at New York

University in the Clinical Social Work Master's program when we discovered our birthdays were one day apart. I was October 15 and she was October 16. We bonded over an impromptu co-birthday trip to Los Angeles for my twenty-sixth and her twenty-third birthday which we both decided was good use of our extraneous student loan funds. We ended up staying at possibly the sketchiest Holiday Inn I have ever encountered, replete with Jurassic sized bugs and a robust sex-for-sale (no judgement, just the facts, ma'am) business which led to some energetic late-night arguments over fees and payments with several customers. We commemorated the celebratory moment of birthdays and friendship beginnings with wrist tattoos from a shop in Venice Beach. In a premonition via inking – of pilgrimages to come, and to be shared—the tattoo I got over that was in simple script on the inside of my right wrist stating, "Every journey is a pilgrimage."

Flash forward from 2006 to 2015 in our friendship and the changes of our lives. Marisol and I had both gotten married in the interim years. Marriages that not only were each of us present for but presided over – she was the officiant for my wedding, and I was the officiant for hers. I had left New Jersey, where we were both living when we met, and was in Southeast Florida. Life, in many ways, was speeding us away from each other, but there was a core to our friendship that had sustained. We had that kind of friendship that just made sense, at a month's notice, to plan to walk Camino together.

I sent her a text one day in the early summer of 2015 and told her I was thinking about walking Camino that August. She and her daughters spent a chunk of the summer with family at their house in Santiago and so it just seemed to make sense that we pair up and make this pilgrimage another collaborative adventure. The plan was simple. Meet in Santiago. Head to the small town of Sarria which served as the last starting point between France and Santiago for the "official" Camino. Que simple. Camino, as pilgrimage of any sort always proves to be, was anything but simple.

So, there we were, starting day take two with me basking in my brazen certainty that, although one day behind schedule, everything was going to only be smooth moving forward.

Get on flight from Barcelona to Santiago—check.

Get off flight—check.

Get to baggage claim—check.

Collect bags—no check.

The absolute absence of a check.

As each bag launched its way out of the gullet of the baggage claim monster each passenger with their matching densely packed Camino-style backpacks grabbed their bags and went on their way. I stared with waning hope into the dark hole that held the secrets to bags come and gone all the way down to the last bag. I looked around and there were still ten of us waiting for our goods to be spit out, each of us wearing the expression between confusion and panic. I began to realize there weren't enough bags for people left. I could see my friend Marisol waving at me from behind the welcome lines. With a big gulp and a hopeful smile I approached her and her awaiting padre for their second day of airports in a row with a smile I hoped didn't allude to the panic out the sides of my mouth.

"Hey! Can you come back here?"

I called out to Marisol and motioned a come here wave, all while smiling with great exuberance at her harried father who was down the mountain to take us to Sarria for the second time in as many days.

As she came through the welcome line to the ugly truth side of baggage claim I begin, "So, here's the thing…none of my stuff is here."

Being us and having been travel companions before through equally ridiculous disasters, we began our trouble-shooting this particular cluster-fuck with a bout of hysterical laughter and luggage-based quips. Like you do. After that subsided Marisol took the lead with her Galician translation to the baggage claim assistant to figure out what was going on at the decisively small and undermanned baggage claim desk. I had lackluster adoptee-level Spanish skills, which folks forget is the same as non-Latinx persons Spanish because I, like them, learned it in high school not at home. As a result, my ability to translate my Spanish into Galician dialect of Spanish found in the region was beyond futile. So, I took my role as smiling sidekick, nodding at what I hoped were the appropriate moments as Marisol took the lead with communication.

We learned one-by-one as each person who went ahead of us did—sometimes when flights are tight on time the airline I lovingly titled "the Spirit Airlines of Spain" would routinely just discontinue loading bags at a certain point. My bag was after that point.

"So," I began, "wait...you are saying they just stop loading bags with bags there? They are just like - eh, too bad?"

"Si," was the succinct response of the nonplussed airline baggage attendant. That one translates from Galician to Spanish just fine.

A note to all travelers from Barcelona to Santiago, never take Spain's version of Spirit Airlines—and as I would also learn—never travel on the first day of the Euro-wide beginning of summer vacation. 'Cause there will always be too many bags.

Marisol, her father and I left the airport leaving a trail of psychotic-level giggling in our wake, because what else can you do? We headed to the family's mountain house in the hills above Santiago proper and not as we planned for Sarria to start the Camino. See, for the Camino, traditionally, you need more than the literal clothes on your back. It's just a good idea.

Once we got to the house a lot of the stages of grief emerged, ones that I realized I would experience in various ways through the Camino and beyond. The longest one this time around was denial. Oh, how strong the denial was in the wake of the loss of everything I thought was essential for my journey. After painstaking months spent planning exactly what was necessary for a Camino traveler. After researching websites and blogs, books and articles, as to what a person would need and what a body was able to carry for a week's worth of walking, there I sat at the kitchen table in the mountains above the city in complete and utter denial of the loss of everything I thought was most important.

Surely my bag wasn't gone.

Surely, I would have things to bring on Camino.

Surely, I wouldn't literally be *going naked* onto the road for a week.

It was amid the laughter and manic tears that bled out that the title for this very book was born—going naked.

Denial seemed to call for something stronger than coffee and so Marisol and I grabbed a bottle of Baileys and a bottle of Albariño—perhaps the greatest white wine of all time and a regional creation—and announced to her parents and her children that we would be upstairs in her bedroom "brainstorming." Brainstorming is what you call getting drunk in the afternoon when there is no other recourse. As denial faded and acceptance seeped in it was clear there was a good chance I was going on Camino with nothing.

The full realization of this possibility became evident after a few calls to the airline customer service during which they explained that due to the holiday backlog it was possible my bags wouldn't be coming for weeks if at all. There were thousands of bags throughout Spain that hadn't made it to their final destinations. All were being held hostage in Barcelona Airport.

Looking out the upstairs window of Marisol's bedroom in a beautiful house in the Spanish countryside I looked towards the front metal gate, standing slightly ajar. After we had reached the house a thick fog had settled on the hillside – coating everything in an almost oppressive level of mist. It was so thick it appeared to have a heavy texture to it, denser than cloud cover, and with a dense scent of rain moving beyond it and through the partially opened window in the upstairs room. The scene was so dramatic it shook something poetic loose in my imagination. Letting something mystical and mythical well inside me. Perhaps delusions of Baileys and "hero's journey" grandeur filled my panicked head, but whatever it was I suddenly had an inspiration for *going naked* on Camino.

If I had to do this pilgrimage with nothing then nothing is all I would need.

As I said this out-loud to Marisol I looked out the window and the thick fog that had coated the entire landscape surrounding us, which had curled up the fence and the walkway to the house obliterating the view of anything beyond the fog itself, began to recede. It moved slowly at first and then, as if with purpose and a place to go, it began to back up in swift strokes, uncovering the walkway to the house, the lines of the fence, the carport and the street beyond until the whole hill was once again visible. It felt like magic. I had spoken words of daring into the oblivion and the unknowing (the space beyond what we know) had answered. The intent of the words and my declaration of moving forward, regardless, had pushed through the unknowing far enough to let me see the next step in front of me.

In this case the next step was: I need a backpack. Marisol's oldest daughter had her school backpack with her from the States. It was one of those fabric Target backpacks from the girls section of the store and we quickly realized we needed to commandeer it. Now, Marisol's daughter, twelve at the time, was no fool. She knew we needed the backpack and needed it desperately and she quickly had a strong bargaining chip.

"So," she began with a shrewdness that made me realize this would not be an easy transaction, "I understand you need this backpack, but you see, I really like it. A lot."

"Yes, Ari, we understand that," I said with all the sincerity I had in me, "and this would be no small sacrifice. You would be giving over this backpack not just to a great adventure but what will become a grand story."

Marisol coming into the negotiations with her words of cajoling, "Ari, this is going to become a book you know, this story, and you, of course would feature in it."

Jumping on this genius of pre-teen marketing I added, "Yes, and of course not only be in it but be a critical character of this story. I mean this backpack is a critical offering to the plot. Without the story can't exist."

Ari stood there, in all her intellectual wisdom and savvy far beyond her twelve years and made a bargain.

"Ok, but I don't want my name just once. I need at least three mentions for this to be worth it."

"Done!" I said with eagerness as we eyed each other and shook on it.

So, this was the negotiation that led to Ariana agreed to give up the sack if only her name—Ariana (also known as Ari)—was mentioned at least three times in this book. Also, as it was clear she was a heroine of this story a secondary condition was that she should and would be clearly articulated as such in the text. And so, as it is clear, so it shall be written. Ariana saved the day and my Camino with her child-sized Target backpack. After the deal was made I made my way around the family house and gathered a few supplies from what Marisol could give up and general supplies from the home like a spare toothbrush and some basic other toiletries. I was ready to start out, naked into the known. While also crossing my fingers against rain. Cloth Target backpacks are not of the waterproof variety.

We left early, the thick mist again coating the roads up above Santiago proper reminding me to heed the warning that even when the way clears temporarily and partially you can't fully know what is ahead. Marisol's dad drove us in the direction of the airport, to yet again ascertain the whereabouts of my wayward bag. I had my plan, my one set of clothes, and my not-weather-proof child's backpack from Target, on loan to me from Ariana, Marisol's daughter—in exchange for a visible role in this book. I was wearing my boots, thank Brown Baby Jesus for small smarts and wearing hiking boots on the plane, and my newly washed old outfit, care of Marisol's wonderfully nurturing mother. Along with what I carried on the outside, on the inside I was sporting a mild hangover care of Baileys and Albariño. The hangover was soon remedied with a stop for café at the local farmland spot which served as coffee shop by day and bar possibly all the time. I was ready to go—backpack or not. I was Camino-bound.

Going Naked would become not just the name of the book but also the fore-telling of things not yet unfolded about having what we need and not what we think we need, about losing everything to realize we need less than we could ever imagine. This was definitively the most hilarious of all the ways I would learn to go naked—with a slim hope that one last check at the airport would proffer my missing bag, I was fully ready to head out with my small cloth bag and nothing else.

When we reached the airport, they looked up the record number from my bag and couldn't find it on site or even in the system as being located, even though the morning flight had come in. The one I had hoped, and they had suggested it might arrive on. Then, as someone opened the doorway to the back room behind the claim counter, Marisol saw a strip of blue and some walking sticks poking out through the crack in the door and shouted, "Aren't those your sticks?!" They were, in fact, my sticks. Apparently, the wrong tag had been put on my bag and had it mixed up with another. Which is also a reminder that, sometimes, when you are willing to go with nothing, and let go of all expectation of something—the unexpected happens and you are given more than you need. Something about 24-hour stripping of my supplies allowed me to see "need" with clearer eyes. I realized I had way too much and before we even left for Sarria I took about ten things out of my bag, determining them totally unnecessary for the journey.

Finally, with beloved backpack in hand we began to drive our way out of Santiago and towards Sarria, our 100-kilimeter pilgrimage starting point. Which, in point of fact ended up being 114-kilometer in total. Why do people round down when you are walking over 100km? It feels like we should be really precise about things like that.

As we drove, backpack crisis of 2015 behind us, the focus became in relaying to Marisol's dad the point of Camino. It made complete sense that to a local Galician the process of Camino was absurd. Jose Lado, not just Marisol's dad but also a native to the mountains we would hike, made some valid points, although not ones we wanted to hear on the verge of a week trekking through the Spanish countryside.

"Pero…I just don't understand why I am driving you away from the house for two hours so you can walk back to the house over five days," he said, forehead scrunched in deep puzzlement.

Marisol then proceeded to explain, "It's a pilgrimage dad, the point is the walking. And part of the journey is stopping along the way to get your Peregrino (pilgrim) passport stamped, as part of the process."

"Well," he said, as if he had figured it out, "if it is about these stamps then that is easy. We will just drive back towards the house and I will park around the corner at these stops. You will get out and get your stamps and then we'll go home. Si?"

We both sighed and laughed in response and explained how the point was not to cheat the system. The point was the walk. It was a spiritual thing, a metaphoric and literal journey. Mostly Marisol's dad just shook his head, mumbling in our general direction in Spanish through the rest of the drive. Two hours later he was no more convinced of our purpose—which I get. If someone asked me to drop them off in Jersey so they could walk to New York City I would probably ask the same questions. I guess "never a prophet in your own country" could also translate to "never a pilgrim in your own countryside." That said, he graciously dropped us at the door of the church in Sarria where we would be able to get our stamp book and our first stamp. We were pilgrims joining at the tail end of what would be for many others an upwards of two-month trek which began in Saint Jean Pied de Port an amazing 764-kilometers from Santiago. Señor Lado helped us unload our bags, laughed a little as he said goodbye, and drove back home to Santiago. We were finally at the beginning of our walking journey. Although starts are never quite as clear as an absolute starting point on a map, made clear by my baggage blunders and Ariana backpack schemes.

We were at the spot on the map where we had intended the journey to begin, in Sarria, the city 114-kilometers from Santiago and exactly the right distance for an "official" pilgrimage trek per existing Camino regulations for Peregrinos (pilgrims). I had to laugh a little when I learned there was a formal process of counting as a pilgrim. The method of certifying pilgrims, and I assume also keeping track of the census as it were of pilgrims completing the walk was two-fold. The first was by authorizing anyone who began the walk in Sarria or earlier to count as an official pilgrim, having completed at least 100-kilometers of the Camino trail. This is specific to the French Route of the Camino as there are now numerous routes with various origin points and lengths for the overall pilgrimage depending on where you start and which route you take.

What is true as a secondary measure of officiating the pilgrim process regardless of your route is the practice of obtaining 2-3 stamps on your pilgrim's passport daily. This passport is a booklet similar in size and format to an actual passport book and the stamps that get marked in your book at designated Camino sites along the way—almost always Catholic churches—are also very similar to actual passport stamps and state the day on which you got the stamp by the volunteer who stamps your book.

This process is the Camino regulators' formula to "prove" you walked the length of the Camino you committed to, which gives you the ability to get what is called the Compostela or the certificate of completion at the Pilgrim's office (run by the Archdiocese) in Santiago. I found the regulation of spiritual process to be one both completely expected of hierarchical religious institutions and hilarious in the conception of an entity micromanaging a mystical process. This is also probably why I never last in institutional processes and systems, particularly spiritual ones. I find the whole conception of managing the divine an oxymoron of epic proportions. While I thought the rhythm to the day such a process would bring, with necessary pauses in sacred spaces, the diploma at the end was by no means my end goal. In truth, my end goal wasn't even Santiago—my pilgrim's path ended in Ávila, where I would revisit the footsteps of Teresa of Ávila. My namesake. My origin story. It also happened to be timed to the 500th year anniversary of Teresa's feast day. So, as I imagined, she and I would have our own little celebration in the walled city of her birth at *my* final pilgrim destination.

FLASHBACK: SACAJAWEA & MARGARET MEAD

While Teresa of Ávila might have been a large part of beginning my life journey the woman I was walking towards from Sarria on that first day of Camino, *who* was walking towards her was something much more complicated. Born in Colombia, a daughter of nuns, brought to the United States by a white American mother and a white British father, I grew up very uneasy in the life I lived and, in many ways in the paradox it held for the skin I grew up in. Who I was, was always an amorphous concept—one that took on an often chameleon-like skin as I found myself acclimatizing for survival to my surroundings. Being raised a brown girl in a white affluent suburb in the New York City metropolitan area it felt like the only way to get by.

As much as I did that though I was always the "never quite" girl. Never quite white, even though I learned the culture, language and traditions of my parent's whiteness and my community's dominant whiteness. Never quite brown, even though the skin I held as I grew into it made it clearer I wasn't related biologically to the family I existed in. I was brown enough to experience the stings of racism, but without the cultural learnings of a family that was equipped to help me through it. Never quite enough—a girl without a country, or more rightly stated, a girl with too many countries, and not enough foundation.

When I was very little, I used my imagination to envision the origins of who I was, beginning pre-verbally with a black and white stencil drawn card glued inside the front of my baby book. It was a woman with dark hair on the background of off-white rice paper with a baby in her arms. For years I envisioned that drawing as my birthmother. Often in toddlerhood and early childhood I would open the baby book to that first page and touch the lines of her face, seeking the familiarity to my own. I would spend hours in the mirror looking over the curve of my nose and shape of my eyes wondering whose they were, wondering whose I was. This question never abated, it just became stronger and more intense. The question of whose we are and who we are is a critical existential question. It is also one that in childhood most are not yet seeking out, because they look above them, and around them, and see the lines of their own face mirrored in the family system that surrounds them. Instinctually and naturally the child then begins to learn the cultural practices of their people, and often hear the languages of their past and their present.

For me it was a foundational question that traveled with me, like the baggage that came with me as I traveled on my first flight at four months of age, from Colombia to the United States.

Who am I?

Whose am I?

While I carried the baggage of that question along with me, through my development of childhood, I also came to the United States and into those formative years, without the necessary supplies needed for the journey I was on.

Who am I?

Whose am I?

As an international adoptee, with the brownness of my skin but without the culture of my people's history, with the Spanish of my name, but the inability to speak the language, I was left in a sort of existential nudity, feeling I didn't have anything to equip me for the journey of myself. I stumbled, lost, learning my way by chance and by misstep, without any maps, without any walking sticks.

When I was about five my parents gave me a set of books called *Value Tales*. They are now out of print, but I retain the two copies of my favorites on the bookshelf in my Chicago apartment because of how formative they were for me in my childhood existentialism. The books were a series of learning tools meant to offer early readers the ability to understand the history and legacy of famous figures and learn lessons based on the identified characteristics of those figures. In each story the figure being highlight would illustrate a certain value through the telling of their life story—and each of the characters always had an imaginary friend, a sidekick of sorts, embodied in some kind of animal. There were forty-three of these tales written but the two that sit on my bookshelf today are the stories of Margaret Mead (who represented the value of under-standing) and Sacagawea (who represented the value of adventure). You could say my whole life could be synthesized into the becoming and undoing of these stories. What was most beloved to me about both characters also took me a lifetime to undo, and in the undoing find the truth of me in both of them, all over again.

What I loved about the story of Margaret Mead was her deep excavation of cul-ture to find a source of truth and her intentionality towards the study of peoples and places she didn't yet understand. Through my childhood vantage point I saw an ability to learn, grow and find community across spaces of newness and a willingness to go to the unknown places without fear. Even at a young age my heart itched for the possibilities across new horizons and ached to learn about people in new places and new ways. I wanted to understand what and who I didn't know and even at that age there was an unconscious seeking of myself in the unknown, as my own personhood was still an unknown place of unknown peoples that I had yet to meet. I thought if I could study enough the nature of people, and if I could learn the cultural lineages of others, one day I would find the moment I felt at home inside myself.

In Sacagawea I saw a sameness that I couldn't describe and didn't yet under-stand. She carried my brown skin and a sense of adventure. She moved between the worlds of brown-indigenous and white people and found a way to not only live in both, but to become an adventurer leading the white community forward while still lifting up her own. I ached for her sense of self, and the understanding of both where she came from and where she found herself, held tightly and proudly as she walked the tightrope I did (blindly) between the worlds of whiteness and "the other." I was in awe of a heroine that I could embrace who I could see myself in. Sadly, to that point, I had not been offered the vision of anyone with brown skin—not in my schooling, or my bedtime stories, or the television shows I had watched. She was the first.

As young as I was, I knew intuitively that I wanted to both hold the ability to study, learn and understand the unknown of myself and my peoples. I wanted to hold a certitude born of being grounded in the being of my ancestors which would allow me to walk in the whiteness of my world assuredly, unafraid of losing myself to it. Margaret and Sacagawea in their idyllic renderings through a caricatured childhood book series made me feel like I could see the path forward a little clearer, and even if I didn't have the tools for the journey, I had some friends who did.

This was also the beginnings of my finding my dearest friends and greatest confidents out of space and time, and often through the pages of stories and the words of authors. Besides the awkwardness of my not-enoughness and my brown-whiteness (or white-brownness) I was also a child who absorbed language with a sponge-like saturation. I spent much of my childhood feeling on the outside of my peers and not all of that had to do with the hybridity of my racial-culture-ethic class. If there had been a superlative that would have fit me throughout my life it would have been, "you use big words." From the time I could talk until well past my high school graduation, I was known as someone who used language that didn't quite fit my age group. I was told hundreds of times by people my age—sometimes with awe, sometimes with annoyance, always with otherness—that I used big words. I wasn't quite sure how to curb this and so I would nestle myself back into the worlds that taught me the big words in the first place. The world of books. The world where my dearest friends and greatest confidents lived.

Beyond that first manifestation of my early literary friends (Margaret and Sacagawea) and these women I aspired towards, I learned over years of work and lots of identity pain, that my early stories of simplistic values, understanding and adventure were also a microcosm of the simplistic white American under-standing of everything I was trying to unearth. While these caricature visions helped give hope to a five-year-old girl, the girl that grew up and out of her had to wrestle with the identities and cultural perceptions of those stories and mythologies which shaped a one-dimensional unhealthy understanding of both those women and me.

What I had learned through the stories that I clung onto as a way to know myself even just a little actually *withheld* the tools of knowing myself and my peoples more than offering them up.

Neither the real Margaret Mead nor the actual Sacagawea fit into the cartoon bubble of history I had been offered. Both of their stories were deeper, and in that depth the relationship between the two was painfully complex. Margaret Mead did build a foundation of understanding indigenous people the world over—but that lens, while female, was white, and in that the viewpoint the western world built of indigeneity was built out of a white framework. This framework simplified and distorted the nature of indigenous peoples, bending it to the will of a woman in a certain time and place, and creating generations worth of work for the peoples of those communities to clear the looking glass and have a voice to talk back into the obscured vision of their identities.

Sacagawea was brave but wasn't the willful adventurer I looked to with hope. She was a child, trafficked by white colonizers as they dominated the land of other peoples (the same kinds of peoples—indigenous—who would later be obscured by the lens of Anglo-anthropology) and forced to travel with her cap-tor, and child rapist "husband," bearing his children and acting as a figurehead of peace for men who meant anything but that. She was brave, but not because she asked to be, because she needed to be to survive.

In this way the story of my childhood became the story of my whole life—this battle to find my place between Margaret Mead and Sacagawea, between the conquered people's histories carried in my brown skin, and the white lineage that would seek to explore them and dissect their beingness.

My whole life has been living between those worlds. Along with living in the in-between I have had to find my place as one raised in a lineage of whiteness, in a conquering nation, while carrying the brown skin of ancestors long drowned out by the conquest. Owning my place between those worlds, between these women in all their complexity, pain, beauty and truth has become what I seek. I didn't travel north in infancy with all the tools in my pack to answer the questions necessary for my journey.

Who am I?

Whose am I?

Even so, the path has been made much richer for the quest to find the tools becoming the dearth of the journey. I still seek, and yearn, undo and rebuild again, this path to who I am and whose I am. I am Margaret Mead. I am Sacagawea. I am also something entirely brand new, bridging between the two and bridging between what is perceived and what truly exists.

FLASH-FORWARD: JUST A HYUNDAI & MY DOGS

Five months after the end of Camino, and one month after the end of my marriage, I pulled out of the driveway of the home I had owned in Boynton Beach, Florida. It was a little yellow ranch with shutters and doors I had painted turquoise blue because it reminded me of Frida Kahlo's house "Casa Azul" in Mexico. In the backseat were my two dogs—Faith (a chihuahua mix) and Gaia (a beagle-corgi mix)—and in the trunk and passenger seat was everything we, now, collectively owned.

I had come back after four weeks on book tour to pack up and leave my home state of the past six years. In full accuracy the first two weeks of the book tour included bouncing around from the Northeast to the Rocky Mountains and the West Coast. The subsequent two weeks were spent in a puddle on my parents' dining room floor staring up at their crocheted picture of the Virgin Mary. Well, not all two weeks did I sit at the feet of the woman I would begin to just call "Crocheted Mary" but she played a prominent feature in the midnight and after hours. It became a creepy late-night ritual between her and I. The kind only curated in the frenetic mania that comes immediately at the end of something big—like a marriage.

It was my first time back to Florida in the full four weeks' and my final time inside the house I had called home. I was coming back to get all my worldly possessions and travel north to Asheville, North Carolina where I would spend the next few months vacillating between puddle status and book tour status—a very precarious dyad—before finally landing in Chicago as my final destination. This would be the first of three times over the next year of packing up my car of just the absolute needs and traveling to the next pinpoint on a map—getting me closer each time to a life I couldn't yet see through the fog of my own despair.

That first move, though, I remember more clearly than all the rest. I remember feeling like everything was moving in slow motion. In the matter of two days and not nearly as many boxes as I would have imagined I packed up what was left of seven years of life with my soon-to-be ex-husband. I shoved what was most precious that would fit inside a Hyundai and drove it out of a marriage and life built in Florida. Those last moments felt profoundly surreal, as the dogs and I slowly backed out of the driveway and away from a marriage, a house, a life owned in conjunction with another. I was leaving behind three of our five dogs which he kept in the split not to mention the house which I am still not sure if it was depression or defeat that made me un-wanting and willing to fight to get even part of in the divorce.

The motion of driving felt necessary and visceral to what I was feeling in my body in that moment because there was nothing solid underneath me anymore, and I couldn't imagine solidity even being possible. If you had asked me before that moment if you could fit an entire life, dogs included, in a Hyundai I would have laughed a hysterical laugh of disbelief at the question. The truth is, when you get right down to it, when you strip away a life of all the things you think you need and want and have for comfort, there isn't much you need to carry.

Little more than would fit in a child's Target backpack, in fact.

When your life is stripped down to non-existence there isn't much that defines the who or whose you are at all.

You have to strip back the layers of all your expectation of what that means and begin again. I had no idea in that moment how absolutely true that was for me and the life I was driving towards. I had spent three days purging and packing, whittling down a life to only its most essential parts. I would later learn that the house itself was already inhabited by someone else's new life—as my husband had moved in his lover, a colleague from his work, before I had even come home to pack. This was unbeknownst to me at the time as she had moved her things out for my last visit back. So, in truth, as I drove away from that house—with the Frida painted doors and the years of memories—I was driving away from a life that already belonged to someone else. Without even knowing that piece of information I felt the truth of it in my gut. Even though the marriage that was ending had been withering and dying for years there was something about being completely without place, without people, without home, ever so slowly and then all at once, that is completely unnerving. I was tether-less in a way that wasn't yet liberating, it just felt like being an astronaut without a ship, stuck in deep space.

I could have never imagined the year previous as I laughed hysterically and filled up that Target backpack how much it was preparing me for the letting go. It was a letting go of the illusion of need rather than want. Letting go of the illusion of comfort as necessity. Letting go of the need for security, the need for tethering for survival. Letting go of the fear of going naked into the world. I learned in the moment I drove out that driveway and every moment after that until I found tethering again, how true that was and how much I needed to learn it.

Letting go is liberation, if you let it be. However, don't forget to read the warning label on liberation and letting go. It will tear you down to nothing but a backpack or a Hyundai first, because you have to lose it all to know you never needed it in the first place. Eventually, over time and through a lot of fear, grief and releasing I found restoration. Much like the return of my backpack in that unexpected moment at the airport, the building of a new life (a new backpack) came again, but the value of losing it all was a gift I never expected.

THE PRACTICE: The Art of Letting Go

The practice for this chapter is to explore what it looks like to let go of what we think we need in order to discover what we really need. Imagine everything you own in this moment—now envision fitting only what you can into your car. Draw it out or write a list of what those things would be. Once you have done that pare it down to just a backpack. Write it out or draw it out. What is left? Why is it important?

Look at everything else you have and begin to consider why you thought you needed it before and why you actually don't need it.

Notice how it feels to let go of what you don't need. Notice the discomfort at what you still cling onto.

Do you feel panic or fear? Do you feel guilt or shame at not wanting to let go? Follow those feelings and see where they lead. Where is the fear or panic coming from—does it go back to your origin story or something else from your past? Where is the fear or shame coming from—what makes you feel guilty about wanting what you don't need?

Journal out this process. This is not just a one-sitting endeavor.

You can bring out your list or drawing for a week or more and see if what you need has shifted—do you need less? See how your feelings or attachments have changed? Do you have less or more fear, shame, guilt or other feelings that emerge? Where are they coming from?

CHAPTER 2

Crossing Over

ON CAMINO: THE BRIDGE

ON DAY TWO of our Camino hike I was a little less exuberant. My foolishly ill-equipped toes were stuffed into brand new and unworn hiking boots which reminded me with every step of acute pain how delusional I had been to not wear them in. My toes and the boots had allied themselves, deciding to prove my foolishness and their protest by searing away the flesh of my pinky toes with vengeance. The hills were steeper on the second day, as well, and I could feel the increasing breathlessness of my body as we climbed up higher and higher into the Spanish hillside. Marisol was already illustrating her soon-to-be unreachable faster pace, as I, my boots, and my trekking poles clumsily plodded along yards behind her.

Damn triathletes!

On this second day, the entry point to the first major town of Portomarín, where we would get our first stamp in our peregrino passport, had a long and tall bridge as the only gateway to the city. It took my brain and body about a third of the way across to realize I was, in fact, on a very high and very long bridge, teetering over a deep and distant river below. Once they did, however, I was incapable of dissuading the panic that began to rise from my feet to my head. I am terrified of heights and always have been. Specifically the fear is targeted at the terror of falling, a theme that has made its appearance in many a nightmare and played itself out, metaphorically, in much of my life.

I got to this point in the bridge where there were limited options. Also, my panicked brain was flooded with all the wonderful hormones that pump through us when we feel fear. It doesn't matter to the brain or the corresponding body responses whether the fear is actual or perceived. Once the system has onboarded fear and danger, it doesn't waver in the abundant pumping of adrenaline, cortisol and all that good energy juice that prepares us to flee or fight. I was frozen in panic, clenching my trekking poles with the whitest of knuckles. Actually, I would like to amend that phrase for a pigment appropriate alternative. I'm brown with olive undertones so let's call it light green knuckling it. Every muscle in my body screaming one word and one word only: abort!

I could go back, I thought, but that would mean turning around and I would still have to walk a good distance in the opposite direction. If I did, though, I could hitch a ride over the bridge.

"Ahem", squeaked my body in a high-pitched voice (as terrified bodies do), "I am not a fan of turning around right now."

As if to make its point, my toes dug deeper into my shoes for emphasis. I took a quick poll of my muscle system from top to bottom: nope. The resounding consensus was nope on going back. My body simply refused to turn that way. I tested it out and it just refused to go back.

First option down, I considered other alternatives. I could walk into the road so as to not be standing on the narrow, grated walkway where I could see the menacing waters below through each and every peephole of terror beneath my toes.

"Excuse me," my brain interjected, interrupting my panicked stream of consciousness.

"I just thought I would point out that there is the likelihood of getting run over by the continuous stream of cars driving recklessly fast as they zoom by."

Ok, I sigh angrily. I had been vetoed already once by my body and once by my brain. Not that either of them had eased up the pumping of stress hormones so I could think any clearer. So much for team-work.

"Alright everyone, last bad option," I mutter to myself.

By this point I was becoming a steady fixture on my personal bridge. I could just stay there, on the bridge, indefinitely. Just set up life in this spot for a while. Not body nor brain seemed to have a distinct argument against this option. I figured we could just set up shop. I would becoming the quirky and slightly odd local bridge lady who muttered to herself while shaking and green-knuckling walking sticks which were gripped to her side in hypocritical mockery of the fact that she never moved, let alone walked.

By this point my travel companion had noticed I was not following behind her. In all honesty the five-minutes that felt like five-hours while I struggled with this life decision I had forgotten anyone else existed in my periphery.

A reminder that no woman is an island, especially not one stuck on a bridge, I heard, through the muffling haze of panic distorting my senses, Marisol shouting, "What's wrong?"

She then made the foolish choice to walk towards me. This was a very bad idea because part of my particular brand of panic had also included the branding this weird isolationist compulsion, cultivated in childhood, to address my private pain and fear alone.

"Don't come near me! Don't look at me! Please, go the other way and don't look back!"

I hear myself screaming out my own manic stream of nonsense before I can come to some more reasonable way to say what I needed. Somewhere in the kaleidoscope of my life's history was this need to not be seen in pain, in fear, in my panic. Like a hurt dog I wanted to hide and tend to my wounds myself, where no one could see them. I had always been certain this was the best way through suffering, and I had been implementing this method my whole life to that moment. The response was so entrenched it was automatic.

"Ok," Marisol said hesitantly with a look that read an additional unspoken, "delusional woman clutching poles on a bridge."

That I was. Still frozen. Still clutching. Staring at the yellow line in the center of the road. I began muttering to myself, "I see the road, I see the cars, I see the road, I see the cars," exactly the way a person becoming unhinged would do. Unhinged and clenching as I was, one third of the way across this very tall bridge, I began to force my legs forward, one step at a time.

"I see the road, I see the cars, I see the road, I see the cars, I don't see anything else," I said over and over again. One step at a time, unwatched and alone, I made my way across the bridge in what felt like hours, but likely was more in the range of five minutes.

Once on the other side of the bridge, after my first steps were taken on solid ground, beyond the watery grave that I had anticipated, I looked up at my travel companion for the first time since I had my psychotic bridge break. Marisol stared at me with a look of concern. Hints of laughter not-so-cleverly hidden at the corner of her mouth. In a couple of breaths my heart stopped racing and I began to smile and then giggle.

"So, yeah, I'm afraid of heights," I said, and we began to laugh, at the obviousness of the statement, and the absurdity of my coping mechanism.

We laughed as we began hiking up an increasingly steep staircase, on our way to the first church stop of the day in Portomarín. I was good at uphill, for some reason. I wasn't impeded at all, as I had feared, by my smoking habit of the last year. I had taken on the habit to stifle the pain of life at home and at work. My life had felt for a while like I couldn't breathe inside of it, and so I had decided to smoke. I had joked to friends at the time that smoking was a breathing exercise with consequences.

Huffing up the hill, still giggling at the absurdity of my outburst, I began to think about what had happened. I was too tired to fully let it settle, but I bookmarked the moment to return to because I knew there was something, not yet reachable, about my literal pushing away of help and privatizing my pain that had deeper meaning for the Camino ahead. The therapist in me also took note, in frustration with the rest of myself not ruled by the years of academic training, that there was something intrinsically unhealthy about hoarding my hurt, both on the road and in my life. Sure, it would eventually get me to the same destination, but at what cost?

FLASHBACK: A SKINNED KNEE

The first time I remember hiding my pain was when I was about ten-years-old, although in retrospect with deeper study I could probably trace it even farther back than that. Likely as far back as the literal hoarding and hiding of food in my room from as early as five-years-old. Something I would learn in adulthood was that hoarding and self-soothing were prototypical responses for children who were in an orphanage in infancy. Infants are fed on a diet of touch as much as food. In a pre-verbal world, the only way they understand their relationship to the world, to caring and survival is through attention. In infancy those are shown through parental touch and the meeting of basic needs (most critically food). Orphanage babies learn to self-nurture due to the lack of consistent attention due to the lack of primary caregivers for each baby, most sharing a room full of other babies. There is no certainty of external caregiving and at a visceral level this wordless language of instability becomes inscribed on the infant psyche, carrying with the child as it grows, even if they are introduced to stable caring later in childhood.

I had learned to self-soothe in infancy, first with thumb sucking, later in toddlerhood and beyond with food hoarding, and continuing in larger and larger ways as I grew into a larger being. I never became willing to fully give over the reins of my needs, my fears, and my self-soothing apparatus to anyone else. That inscribed intuition that my survival and nurturing was up to me, and to hand it over was a dangerous proposition was something I had written and rewritten all over my life without consciously realizing it. Even when I would learn the psychological mechanics of this kind of attachment disruption, studying trauma in graduate school and doing my own self-study on the subject, I was never able to unwrite the narrative that was written in my gut.

Specifically, when I think back to how entrenched this pattern of behavior was, I remember a single experience from when I was ten. It is one that I began to reflect back on as I looked at myself more closely for the pattern of making my pain private. I had been at the park down the road from my house, with my siblings and my father. We were riding bikes around the racetrack that made up half of the park. It was the middle of a particularly sticky New Jersey summer, just as sunset was peeking through the trees lining the edge of the field. I lost my balance. Losing balance was a lifelong habit of mine and I fell hard onto the gravel track below. I looked down as blood began streaming down my leg from my kneecap and I could see where big chunks of gravel had imbedded themselves into my flesh.

My next-door neighbor, Mrs. Brown, a middle school home economics teacher with a lifelong penchant for nosy neighboring was standing across the field from me and came running over.

"Are you ok, dear? Do you need help?"

It was one of the few times I remember seeing her as nurturing, but even as I heard her words, and felt their sincerity, I could feel my body recoil away from her outstretched arms and concerned stare. I felt exposed and I just wanted to escape to somewhere where no one would see me, my pain or my blood-drenched knee.

"No, I'm fine," I said, fumbling to pick up my bicycle, feeling the sting as the immediate surge of adrenaline began to fade. Burning pain was beginning to emanate from the center of my leg and downward, all the way to the nerves in my toes.

Without even looking back, I began fighting against the heavy gravel to thrust my bike forward in the direction of home. I didn't tell anyone I was leaving; certain Ms. Brown would take care of informing my dad and surrounding neighbors in the park. The beneficial side of the nosy neighbor was she was always sure to pass along information. My only goal was getting home. I distinctly remember making all efforts not to limp, afraid passersby would see me struggling and offer similar discomforting words of help. All pain must be hidden. All signs of it must be secret.

"I just want to get home," I remember thinking.

"If I can get home no one will be able to see."

I rushed up the steep driveway of my mountain road home, shoved the bike down next to the garage, and ran in the front door. By this point I could feel the blood soaking into my socks and onto my shoes. My mother stared at me as I noisily blew open the screen and glass door, scrambling to get to the bathroom. The bathroom was my safe zone.

"What happened?"

My mother squealed at me in her concerned voice, which always managed to get three octaves higher than her speaking voice, piercing my ears and alarming my already alarmed panic system. I was consumed by trying to ignore the level of pain in my leg while still making every effort not to show a sign of weakness by limping.

"Nothing. I'm fine," I mumbled, as I ran into the hall bathroom and locked the door.

I immediately turned on the shower, stripped down, and jumping in, trying to blot out my mother knocking on the door.

"Teresa, let me in. I can help," she said with such concern I momentarily felt guilty for locking her out of my pain.

"No, I'm ok. I can handle it," I said as I began pulling gravel out of my knee, one painful gray clump at a time.

It was excruciating. I remember crying tears that seemed to be connected to my pain sensors more than my will. No matter how hard I tried to stop them from coming, the tears dripped down my face, concealed in their fervor only by the intensity of the water stream spraying from the shower head. I spent close to an hour in that bathroom and in that shower, with the door locked, blood spilling down my leg, as I dug into my knee pulling out thick gravel one piece at a time. I cried and groaned but, intentionally, never loud enough that it could be heard over the shower spraying over my body and washing away the blood as it fell.

Door locked, in the darkness, plucking out the painful interloper of hurt and pain I was creating a hallmark. I was building a methodology I would employ throughout my life of concealing that which hurt me the most, holding it close to me, and never revealing it until it was a distant memory. After the hour that felt like an infinity had passed, sunset having moved across the sky and transforming into the cooler darkness of a summer night, I made my way out of the bathroom, dressed my wound and made my way down for dinner.

"I'm ok," I thought. "Now I am ok. No one had to see."

I walked into the kitchen, intentionally smiling, as if nothing had ever happened.

FLASH-FORWARD: L.A., TEARS & NAKED PAIN

My marriage ended on a balcony in Redondo Beach, California just after sunrise one weekday morning. I had traveled the thousand or so miles across the country as part of the launch for my second book, *Sacred Wounds*, and had, the day before, finished both my session on healing woundedness as well as a lively late night podcast during which my "fake birthday" was celebrated in a room with about fifty live viewers, singing at the top of our lungs, *Free Falling* by Tom Petty. A personal favorite. The irony of that song, the last act of the last night before my marriage ended, would become almost synonymous with that balcony experience.

I remember the stucco on the side of the motel which housed the balcony on which I sat. It was rough like the stucco on my home in Florida, and the color was burnt orange. The balcony floor where I was sitting, sprawled out, and looking a mess, was littered with dozens of my cigarette butts. My survivalist habit I had appropriated over the previous year to deal with the immense sadness and loneliness inside my relationship, and dissatisfaction in my life going strong the previous night into the early morning I found myself in. I was sucking in hard as much carcinogen as I could, practicing my breathing exercise with consequences. However, right in that moment I wasn't even thinking about the consequences. I just thought if I sucked in the smoke fast and hard enough it would somehow stop the endless number of tears dripping down my face. It wasn't doing the job, but I was a pack and half in and not ready to give up the experiment.

My marriage ended on a balcony in Redondo Beach, just outside of Los Angeles proper, 2,691-miles away from my Florida home, and over the phone. I knew we would end. I knew it would be soon. Part of me knew when I left for my four-week-long book tour to launch *Sacred Wounds* that we might not be together by the time I got back.

As I sucked down smoke I thought, "But not like this. Not on the balcony of this motel at the furthest point I could possibly be from home."

The choice to do it that way at that time hadn't been mine. Although I begged my husband to wait until I got home—the therapist in me wanting to process this in some way that was salvageable as healthy—where we could do this in front of a therapist.

"At least let me come home now. We can't do this over the phone."

He refused. He told me to stay away the additional week and a half I had left on my tour telling me, "We won't be able to do it if you come back; we'll just end up staying together. Plus, you'll be with your friends, you'll be fine."

The former statement was quite possibly true, even so, it was a pretty shitty way to end a marriage—over a continentally divided cell phone call. The latter was one of those finite digs at the work that kept me on the road with people other than him—part of some of the last straws which had been pulled off our fragile broken marriage over the last year.

I had no idea where I would go, all I knew was that my next speaking gig was taking me to New Jersey, just by grace and chance, the place where my parents were, and that I would figure the rest of life out from there. I would also do it annexed from my home of the last six years—a home that I didn't even know, from this point on, if I was allowed to call home.

My brain was on traumatic stress overload—I couldn't think a straight thought; I couldn't make a straight plan. All I knew was I had to get to New Jersey, and I had a flight leaving LAX later that day that would do just that. My colleague, Harriet, with whom I was sharing the Redondo Beach Motel, came outside onto the balcony, having heard the phone call. She looked down at me and the emotionally naked mess of rubble I was—in my pajamas, strewn out on concrete, smoking the crap out of my pain.

"What happened?" she asked.

"My marriage is over," I squeaked out, the words not yet making sense to my tongue as they rolled out into the air.

I know Harriet helped me with the process of collecting myself and my belongings out of that motel and into the car and I can remember her driving us back to the venue where we had been the night before, as well as kindly offering to run inside and get what remained of my books—the ones that hadn't sold during the conference. Never before had I wished harder that I wore sunglasses, having nothing but the car window as protection between my tear drenched face, puffy eyes, and the world.

"Please, please, please," I thought as loudly as I could in my mind, "No one see me, and please, don't let anyone come over here."

Almost predictably so, the second that Hail Mary of a prayer left my lips I heard furious knocking on my side of the car. It was the vendor for my books and, of course, her small child waving to me with only a sheet of glass and some car metal between us.

"Oh, God," I thought, "I am going to have to get out of this car."

I put on the most speedy and believable smile face I could muster and opened the car door. Her level of chipper in that moment almost sent me right back inside the door, safely away from all the human people living their lives which didn't involve a total life rupture.

"Hi! So, it was so great to have you with us! I have those books for you, can you wait here?"

"Oh, sure, of course," I said, "I think Harriet went in to find them for me."

She began to walk away, and I thought, "Ok, I did that, and I didn't have an emotional break, at least now I can get back in the car."

Of course, as soon as I said that, and my hand reached the door handle and the safety behind glass and metal I heard, "Teresa, hey!" It was the voice of one of the conference organizers coming up behind me. I plastered back on what felt like an overdoing-it-grin and stared at him, not sure if more words were going to come out of my mouth.

"Yes, I had a great time, it was great," I said with the overdone smile unmoving and mechanically held by what felt like a mixture of plaster and grace.

"Yeah, it has been so wonderful having you here. We would love to have you back again."

"Yes, great. I had a great time, it was great." I said again, hoping that I was playing it cool and my repetition of the exact same words hadn't aroused suspicion of an impending tear explosion that I felt coming on like a sneeze you can't stifle.

He walked away and I took a deep sigh, thinking, "Thank God, at least now I can get back in the…"

"Hey, Teresa," called out the podcast host from the night before, "That was a great fake birthday wasn't it? And singing "Free Falling" together, so great!"

"Yes, it was great, I had a great time, it was great," I said, hoping I hadn't done one too many greats while I plastered the Cheshire cat grin back on my face, feeling like an escaped psych patient, just trying to get out of the institute before anyone noticed my disguise as a person not about to lose their mind.

I got back in the car just in time for Harriet to return with my books saying, "Hey, what were you doing out of the car?"

"Trust me," I said, "If I could have avoided it, I would have," as the tears began to spill back out of my eyes, having waited as long as they could to return.

As a point of reference—I was not a public crier. Ever. While some people have that repeated dream of showing up to class with no clothes on, my equivalent nightmare would be showing up in tears. Since that skinned knee at ten, and probably even before, it was just something I didn't do. My tears were always private, the people who had seen them come out were rare and few, and to that point in life it had been limited only to my immediate family and my husband. My tears, my pain, was my secret thing, which I shared as little as humanly possible—feeling exposed or weak if anyone caught a glimpse of them. I had a pretty good track record. Up to that point I couldn't think of a single incident in the last decade preceding that day in which I cried to or in front of anyone else. Maybe part of it was training and years of practice as a trauma therapist, hearing the most painful and horrible things of other people's lives, or my own experience of hardening and staving off direct feelings after moving through and out of my own battle with Post-traumatic Stress Disorder in my twenties subsequent to sexual trauma. Maybe it was the little girl who learned to run and lock the door before crying—so that her pain could be private, controlled and her own. Likely, it was all of those things, but whatever the combination of sources there were only a literal handful of people who had ever seen me cry and the inability to escape the flow of tears at this moment, in that pain, like a tornado of hurt, was as maddening and terrifying as the circumstances that had created their release from isolation.

I realized quickly that the suddenness and depth of my pain disallowed me from employing my old mechanisms of private pain and isolation. That and being in the most public environments possible. First, the encounters at the conference center and then, immediately following that, being at an airport. The tears were unstoppable. No matter how many times I pretended I had something in my eye, they kept rushing out, making any attempt to stall them looked absurd. The traumatic intensity of the pain forced it to go live and public in a very big way. It was the most uncomfortable, disarming and uncontrollable thing I had experienced. I could feel the sheer force of my pain pulling itself out of the depths of me and bringing it front and center into the world, the one place from which I had always shielded it.

On arrival at the airport I realized I was about to be stuck on a plane with my eye-leaking compulsion on super drive, stuck besides strangers for the longest flight distance one could have in the continental United States—Los Angeles, California to Newark, New Jersey.

"Of course," I thought, "Because anything else would just be too easy."

I was then seated in the middle seat, wedged between a mother and a daughter who proceeded to chat for the bulk of the flight, right over my writhing body, combusting with salty ocular discharge that had never had this kind of public exposure. I kept wiping my eyes, continuing my futile attempt to pretend I had something stuck in them, but by hour five that seemed to be the weakest and most ridiculous of lies, even to me. To my benefit, perhaps, my newly naked and exposed pain seemed to be completely unseen by my neighbors to my left and right as they continued to talk away. They chatted over my mourning body like they were in a coffee shop and I was the umbrella stand between them. It is a surreal feeling to cry the length of the United States, but it is equally surprising when no one notices. That said, even with their indifference, I was deep into public exposure discomfort. I felt like an emotional flasher, compulsively exposing myself and my pain, hour after hour, to a cabin full of passengers with no escape for any of us.

We were winding into the last leg of the flight, my body exhausted, my muscles cramping from the spasms of crying and the attempts at diminishing the spastic movement when the pilot came on the intercom.

"Alright everyone. So, there is some kind of electrical issue with the tower in Newark. We are not sure what it is or when it will be fixed so we're going to go ahead and reroute to Chicago and land there…I am not sure what we're going to do after that."

"Um, yep. That sounds about right," I thought.

On par with the worst day of my life.

Of course, we would reroute to Chicago as I was encased in a prison I couldn't escape. I was utterly exposed in all my messy tearfulness, blurry-eyed from crying, with no way to make this nightmare end.

"Yep, let's go to Chicago. I can't think of any other way to make this more uncomfortable than it already is than an indefinite landing in a city and state nowhere near my destination."

While we sat on the tarmac at Chicago O'Hare airport my two travel buddies began chatting and moving around, and the lights came blasting on.

I suddenly had an image of the wolf in *Little Red Riding Hood* in my brain saying, "For the better viewing of your nervous breakdown, my dear."

Exactly three minutes before I got up, with the totally rational plan in my head to insist I be let out of the plane so that I might find the nearest hotel and cloister up with bourbon and private crying for an unknown amount of days, the captain came back on the intercom.

"Ok, everyone. Whatever was going on at Newark is fixed and so we're going to go ahead and take off again for our final destination."

"Thank you sweet Brown Baby Jesus!" I thought with as many exclamation points on that statement as my mind could muster.

The only thing that might feel slightly more pathetic than crying your way across the country is waiting at the baggage carousel as the luggage goes round and round, publicly weeping in a common area, then lugging said baggage off the carousel, wiping the snot which at this point was a futile and ridiculous effort, and dragging what is all your current life belongings to the curb to wait for pickup. By the time my parents arrived, the only thing I had the energy to do was collapse in their car. I was not able to unpack any of the baggage of the last day, but I left the day behind knowing that I would be unpacking a heavy load the next day and days to come. I felt a small twinge of accomplishment at having exposed my pain and knowing that it would not kill me to do so.

All my thoughts were still a blur and I didn't really understand, yet, what I was beginning to uncover—or how the weight of the greatest pain made and would continue to make me expose it in ways I didn't think I ever could, to people who cared, and people who loved me in expected and unexpected places, not despite but because of the authenticity of my hurt. In that moment I was glad to roll into bed, spoon a big pillow, and sob between nightmares and panic attacks—which would ensue the next couple of weeks—at the complete collapse of my life as I had known it for nearly a decade.

By exposing my pain in that first obscene and public way, through my continental breakdown, I began to realize that I had privatized and compartmentalized my pain as one of my core compulsions for a lifetime. I had spent my life hoarding it, and the more pain there was the deeper and more completely I hid it. In the last year or so of my marriage, more completely than ever before, drowning in the pain, I stuffed it down as far as I could. I had reached a peak of pain avoidance, not even giving tears to myself in private, let alone in public. In doing so, I had begun to live a sort of half-life, where my greatest truth, my pain, was tucked away and stuffed down for no one to see and holding onto it was slowly poisoning my soul. A soul cannot survive only half alive and invisible. I had become like Gollum from *The Lord of the Rings*, internally possessive of that which was mine and mine alone - my precious suffering.

As a result, nothing in my life was really real and my authentic-self had begun to disappear. But when divorce ripped my private pain out from my secret hiding place and the hurt was so great I couldn't avoid being exposed, I found this miracle. Notwithstanding my initially ignorant plane companions, I began to find all these beautiful people willing and wanting to listen to my pain, hold me close, and let me cry and cry out without censoring the suffering. In that I found a gateway to personal liberation and collective union I didn't know was possible and had never experienced to that extent before. Beloved community created itself around me—in strangers, acquaintances, and surprising new friends who saw my whole self because I exposed my pain, and loved me in and through it and because of, *not* in spite of it. I didn't know if I had ever before felt such radical acceptance as I did following the end of my marriage.

It was truly miraculous. Letting my whole-self show did make me more vulnerable, but unlike in the prison of my pain, in the worst last years of my marriage, I didn't feel unhealthily exposed or lonelier for the exposure. I felt comforted with the truth of love that was limitless. It was as if the divine had found me in the one place I least expected it and the one part of myself—the epicenter of my pain—which I had not shown to the world for fear it would break me apart. In truth, it did break me apart, but in that way that liberated me from the solitude of suffering and scattered the pain onto the ground. The pain wasn't gone, but it was no longer held inside the prison I had made of my soul. It freed my soul to start a new journey of becoming my whole self, much as being liberated from unhealthy relationship had painfully broken me open, too, to be the fullness of me. Uncertain what that looked like at least I could finally begin to walk forward in greater lightness of baggage. One more thing removed from my spiritual backpack that I no longer needed to carry—my privatized hidden pain.

In the days following my divorce, sequestered at my parents' house in New Jersey, I had nothing to do but see and feel my feelings and do a lot of crying. I began to see the gateway to this liberation of truth from hurt. I cried tears of grief and loss. Even an unhealthy relationship, when lived in for so long, is a loss, like a death. I had not realized how deep or palpable the pain would be or how beautifully welcome and welcoming the kindness of listening ears and gentle words would become.

My Camino friend Marisol, having recently gone through her own paradoxically long-time-coming and also traumatically-abrupt divorce, came over one day and took me on my first real date in a long time. She surprised me with a beautiful dinner and an evening of painting and wine at a local paint-by-numbers place in Jersey City. It felt good to be home. To be loved. To be seen. In a way I had not felt in years. I painted a terribly pathetic looking replica of a lighthouse that I named, totally irrelevantly and irreverently "The Great Divorce" after both my own impending divorce process and the book by C.S. Lewis of the same name which felt apt. The book explores the process of escape from purgatory.

The lighthouse itself stood as a beacon of a safe place to land on the horizon. It was hope. It was the possibility of my truth shining brighter out of darkness and my soul no longer stuck in its own claustrophobic purgatory I had kept it in for too many years. And it marked the first day I had gotten out of my pajamas in a week—so I also felt pretty good about that. Clothing oneself again is always a good sign. And bathing, which I also did for the first time in a week, that same day. So, liberating the soul through authentic relationship and bathing—it was the first step on a long road out of grief and into liberation.

THE PRACTICE: Finding Your Bridge Place

The practice for this chapter begins with drawing an image of a bridge.

Then place on that bridge the imagery or language which represents your own fears or roadblocks which are currently holding you back from moving forward on the path you feel called to move along.

At the far end of the bridge you can draw/write the motivations you have for reaching the end of the bridge.

What makes you want to take each step, through the fear, despite the fear, towards what you want? What helps you keep focused on moving forward?

Then, at the other end of the bridge, at the beginning, put the words/images for whatever is pulling you back in the other direction.

What is making you want to stop, give up, or what makes you want to just go backwards and give up the journey altogether?

Reflect on these three elements of this "bridge place" related to your current journey of life—what is calling you backwards, what is stalling you out where you are, and what is motivating you to move forward.

Part of a continuing hope chest project will be to continue to add more on the motivation list and begin to add words, objects and images that reflect that motivation to the existing physical hope chest.

ALTERNATIVE PRACTICE: Seeking & Seeing Your Private Pain

What part of yourself do you hide from others? What are you afraid of sharing with another person? What holds you back from being your whole and authentic self in the presence of another? Where do those barriers come from? What is their origin place?

PRIVATE PAIN RITUAL:

1. *Write a letter to someone you might be willing to share that hurt with, exposing the pain by writing it down.* It doesn't mean you will send or

hand that letter off today. Maybe you aren't ready yet and that's ok. Write it with the intention of sending it to that person.

2. *Take a personal inventory of what things or fears are holding you back from sending it & the benefits that could come if you did send it.* You can do this by making two columns on a sheet of paper. In one column list your fears and hesitations about sending your letter. In the other column write down the benefits or positives that could come from sending it. Every day return to the letter and reread it. When you do, go back to your list and uncover at least one new benefit from sending the letter. Do this each day until you are ready to send your letter. Do this until the benefits outweigh the fears so much that you begin to feel the liberation of what sending it will offer to you more than anything that is holding you back.

3. *When you are ready, send the letter.* Free yourself from the prison of your private pain by offering it up and making it visible.

The monsters in our closets are always more terrifying when they are kept locked up. We make them bigger and more frightening behind that door—our imagination running wild with the visions of their terror and the fear of opening the door and unleashing their ferociousness. What we find when we open the door is usually a shadow masquerading as a monster; it is hollow and weak and not a monster at all. When we liberate our pain we find that it didn't kill us, and it didn't weaken us to show it—it actually made us stronger and more durable. Now we know the monsters are just shadows we're too afraid to face. When we do face them, their power over us evaporates like the trick of light and shadow that they really are and always were while we kept them locked behind that door. We also learn that taking that one heavy thing out of our interior backpack makes the travel forward so much easier.

CHAPTER 3

Alone-Together

ON CAMINO: RHYTHM OF THE ROAD

I HAD GONE on Camino with the expectation of a *Wizard of Oz* band of travelers—broken, fragmented, with our own specific parts missing. I imagined the walk would bring us together, like a band of misfits, and would be something done together. Simple human physiology, once on Camino, taught me differently. We all have a different pace, a different rhythm, different bodily strengths. In my case, I had a dearth of physical weaknesses. My travel companions, people known and unknown to me before the journey, had their own baggage, their own journey, and their own rhythm and pace to their Camino. This was something I learned in fits and starts on day one and with full clarity saw the impact on the walk by day two.

The journey of the Camino was far more solitary than the *Wizard of Oz*, or than the "gringo" (as my taxicab driver called it in one Camino town) adaptations of the pilgrimage like the movie *The Way* would have told us and hit each pilgrim differently. I can only say what I saw externally in how my fellow travelers responded to the enforcement of solitude on the road. I wonder now if it is a reflection of how we deal with the journey of life or the pilgrimage into the self as a whole.

One woman I encountered and spent some periodic time with along the way seemed to become angry and sullen—almost angry at others around her for the inability of the trip to look the way she had envisioned it. She lashed out and alienated others because she so desperately wanted to rail against the pilgrimage she hadn't planned for and variable solitude of the days. My friend Marisol took a hiker's approach to the transition from a collective journey to individual rhythm and plowed ahead of the crowd with trekking poles flying and her boots synching up with the fittest and fastest in our cluster of travelers.

I, on the other hand, went through a variety of internal emotions. First, I had my requisite rage at my body that I had found myself having so often in the previous decade of life. When, on so many occasions, it had failed to live up to the life I wished it could live and the expectations I had for it based on my age and the "supposed to" of its capabilities I would get so angry at my body as if it were a separate entity working against my own needs. This was followed by frustration and feelings of alienation from the journey of others, as if somehow, a few miles up the road, there was a big ol' festive gaggle of travelers building community and making memories that I would never experience. This inherent feeling of "missing out" on some myth of pilgrimage that never existed hit me hard but began to fade by the end of day two. Then there was the grief and letting go of all the expectations of what this trip would look like and what pilgrimage should be. Which quickly reminded me of what I used to tell my therapy clients all the time: don't should all over yourself. Eventually, like stages of grief, by day three, there was an acceptance of this unexpected cadence of travel. I began to find my own way of doing Camino, one that fit my body, mind and soul uniquely. I got into the rhythm of days spent with the soundtrack in my iPhone, the shuffling of my dilapidated body, and the insistence of the horizon to make it just a few more miles to the next albergue (hostel) over the next Spanish hillside. Once I accepted the rhythm of life that was the road of yellow arrows which marked the way to go, I was able to find the hidden togetherness inside the solitude of the Camino's journey. I realized that while I was separated from the intended shared space with my own companions the road was full, every day, with travelers, each one fellow pilgrims, walking beside me. Through canopied forests, long stretches of fields, and the ridges and peaks of the Gallego terrain—with its ancient Celtic roots and unfamiliar dialect—hundreds of us pack-wearing travelers walked together. Alone-together became the term I gave this massive and collective rhythm of life we shared. We were strangers who became familiar to each other over time. There was a consistent plotted course built into everyone's peregrino map no matter which guide book you got your map from, and distinct distances between each start and end town for each day of travel. Due to this, I soon realized that these hundreds of strangers that walked beside me daily—sometimes far ahead, sometimes behind—were the same people that filled up the same towns as I did at night. They also stopped at the same cafes for breakfast and lunch spots when the midday sun became so intense that even the hiking champions had to stop for food and water. The rhythm of life on the road was made up of this wide community of people, walking our own solitary pilgrimages, but also doing it together.

Like other communities there were a variety of subcultures. There were the older women who walked without packs—being part of tour groups that carried people's packs town-to-town—and would maneuver past me, swinging their arms in sync like mall walkers in middle America. There were the young backpacking hikers, who saw more of a physical challenge than a soul's journey in the terrain of the Camino. They often led the pack with a fury that felt almost manic at times. There were the cyclists who seemed like adventure junkies as they sped past, often in matching shiny cyclist suits—looking like competitors on the Tour de France. There were the sweet couples, old and young, on either ends of marital landmarks from newlyweds to forty-year anniversaries, often softening their gait to hold hands and walk in step with one another. There were the noisy high school groups full of adolescent boys who sped through the pathways, often seeming like they barely saw their surroundings as they shouted jokes at each other, making everyone else wish they would speed on by faster. Occasionally, I would see a mirror person to me, a younger person walking alone, stopping often, with some kind of physical pain slowing them down. Like me they would adjust and readjust whatever they could to ease the discomfort, even a little, and then make their way, un-rushed, forward down the path.

Finding the community in the midst of my solitude made it easier to slow down and take care of myself. Something I hadn't thought to do for a very long time. Not just on Camino but just as much in life I hadn't really thought what

I needed or about the particular ways to nurture the body I lived inside of and alongside. I started to find moments to take a long rest under a shaded tree, and not worry about how many people were passing me by. In some ways it was the beginning of a lesson that would continue to unfold in my life ahead—learning to listen to myself, inside and out, and learning to find the space to be alone, and find the beginnings of peace in that solitude. Every day I would wake up with an idea of what the day would look like and by evening, which was like a year of life later in Camino time, I would have learned something unexpected. By sunset daily I'd have moved through some deep and unforeseen emotional baggage, and I did it alone-together—with the community walking beside me through my solitary struggle.

I also learned that often when you think you are walking the journey with certain folks, like those I began my Camino alongside, you find yourself walking with a very different community of support when it's all said and done. Sometimes who we start the journey with is not who we are meant to move through our whole story with or end a particular phase and place of life with, and that, in itself is both a process of grief and letting go. I had to let go of who and what I expected those companions to be on my journey and learn that the story would never look exactly how I envisioned it when I started. This is one of the true lessons of pilgrimage. What we expect is rarely what happens, and relationship changes dramatically in the pilgrim seasons of our life. Sometimes indefinitely. Sometimes irreparably. Sometimes temporarily. We can never really know when we start how it is going to end. A teacher and soul friend of mine, Tessa Bielecki, another beloved of Teresa of Ávila, and author of Teresa-related books, said something at a conference we were both speaking at that summarized this learning curve of life transitions and pilgrim paths for me so succinctly.

She said, "Grief rewrites your address book." She followed this by referencing the nature of life and difficult journeys saying, "Death is for life—another lesson from the compost pile."

Alone-together on the road. Alone-together at home. Pilgrimage teaches us the same things on mountaintops and in the depths of the valleys of our lives on the home front. Grief rewrites your address book—and sometimes your travel plans. Sometimes the road offers us the opportunity to grieve—our expectations of ourselves, of others, of the journey—and in the process it rewrites everything.

However, alone-together perseveres. We are never fully alone, even when we walk in the solitude of our own struggles, carrying our own personal packs of baggage. This knowledge allows us to keep going. It kept me going, each and every mile beyond what I thought I could possibly do. I couldn't have done it alone—the community helped to carry me over each and every ridge, and across each and every hillside. We all did it, like a tidal wave and a forceful breeze, always moving alone-together.

FLASHBACK: REWRITES & ADVENTURES

The grief and loss of the expected versus the unexpected adventures has been a phenomenon plaguing me since childhood. On Camino I realized, not necessarily for the first time, but perhaps the first time I didn't actively fight against it, how powerful the anticipated dream ruled my life and how often I let that incapacitate the joy of the unexpected adventure—most especially when it came to relationship with others.

From as early as I can remember, as far back at least as Smurf cartoons and Mr. Rogers "Land of Make Believe" I had this pesky habit of taking reality or fantasy and rewriting it until it fit the needs of my level of drama, intrigue and human connection. Whether it was an episode of *Teenage Mutant Ninja Turtles* or an interaction on the playground I wanted to rewrite the world towards my own aspiration of perfection. I would rewrite and rewrite the script of life in my brain until I completely expected the next act of life's play to meet the lines on the scripted page. I wanted it to look how I wanted it to look, which was usually some version of happily ever after.

I think some of the greatest sufferings in my life, the hardest moments that made me have to stretch the limits of my own capacity and sanity, also forced me to move out of the scripts of what I wish would be and face the true reality of life: my sexual traumas in my late teens, my panoply of medical issues beginning in my twenties, an irreparable marriage into my thirties. The script of the real pilgrimages of life, the hurt places and the deep journeys not only didn't follow the script I had assigned them, but they required me to face the dimensions of pain I would never have consciously written into any happy ending.

When I was in kindergarten my teacher told my mother at a parent-teacher meeting, that she thought I was autistic because of the amount of time I spent staring off, distracted from the classroom and into some kind of alternate state. The truth is, if anything, I was just idealistic and with a very runaway imagination to carry my idealism forward. This inherent nature made reality feel boring at best and exhausting at worst in comparison to the machinations in my head. But whether slightly autistic or idealistic to my teacher, a person cannot live inside the imagination rabbit hole I had squirreled away my aspirational world. I spent much of my life trying to do just that and finding disappointment with reality as a result. It was never *enough*.

On Camino, though, I was reminded or possibly shown for the first time, that not only is my story and my solitary journey enough, but I don't have to walk it alone. It hurts, a lot, and often—the emotional, physical and spiritual pain of the real journey is unavoidable—but it is mine. Not only that but I can, in fact, walk the path. Each step I *have* taken myself, the real me, not some figment in an idealized world. The real me has walked through the hard places: the me with an often-defunct body, sometimes overeager emotional landscape, and with a spiritual pathway filled with exceptionally rocky terrain. This is the life I am called into and I can actually live into it if I keep my feet on the ground, walk ahead, and remember one step at a time makes the journey.

While I can still find myself flitting into the fictional adventure-land crafted behind my eyes, I find it more of a hobby these days than an occupation. It seems the work is intended to be done on the visceral plane—where feet walk, and where dreams are manifested in messy and haphazard ways, often proceeded by intense and painful roads. We are called to live in this land we call life, where there are no rewrites.

The truth is that when we live out the story that is our own authentic journey we find that the people on our alone-together path emerge who we were meant to find. Which is so much better than anyone we could contrive in a vision of who we want in our lives. Kurt Vonnegut, in one of my favorite books of his, *Cat's Cradle*, talks about something he calls the "karass." For years when I disavowed my Christianity and decided to create a spiritual ethos made up of lyrics and literature—a mix of my favorite fictional metaphors along with Ani Difranco and Indigo Girls songs—I found deep comfort in the spiritual principles of the karass. So much so that I spent much of my twenties describing my spiritual philosophy with this idea as the core premise.

The karass, as I interpreted it, was a group of people, of unknown number, with whom we are eternally connected. Some of them we would meet for an hour and some we would know for a lifetime, but they would be called into our lives, in different seasons, on different parts of the journey, for different reasons and in various ways. They were part of us though, like communal DNA, that we carried with us and were just waiting to be activated. Now of course the imaginative idealist in me loved the poetry of this and the cosmic symmetry. How often I wrote and rewrote characters I thought should play an important role in my life, who I wished would be part of my karass. That said, I was always wrong, because we can't script out our fellow pilgrims or manifest when they should show up. The mall jogging women and the zealous cyclists of our life show up when they are called and how they are called, and we can't predetermine that with any level of imagination.

That is the beauty of the road—we cannot script who shows up.

That is the magic of pilgrimage. Our karass comes to us as our life does, which is what I didn't understand when I was crafting the Vonnegutesque spirituality of my early twenties. Vonnegut was on point, I still believe, just not the way I imagined it or any way I could have imagined it. Alone-together is life's unfolding of the karass, and I never could have written the story as intricate, whole, or diverse as life did.

Life wrote in Grey nuns, and Spanish saints, love and broken heartedness, all in unexpected places. Life wrote a pilgrimage that would birth me from Teresa and lead me back to her down a Spanish trail heading towards her decades later. In that way I am reminded that life is always a series of incidents along the path of alone-together. For me, Teresa of Ávila, has been my companion along that road, when I saw her and when I didn't. When I walked slow or fast or fell down altogether. She was both invisible and visceral and even when I was alone, I always knew we were together. She was my life Camino companion who was there before I knew it and has never left my side.

FLASH FORWARD: WILD WOMEN, WILD HORSES

It was a month after my travels to Spain and I was sitting in an Airbnb in Albuquerque, New Mexico. The day before had been the commencement of a two-year program I had participated in called the Living School, a new program of the Center for Action and Contemplation with Father Richard Rohr, Cynthia Bourgeault and James Finley. I had decided to stay on after the graduation day at the invitation of some of my female classmates who were spending a few days post-graduation in Albuquerque to decompress and languish in a mystic commune type of experience which had been refreshingly present through our yearly symposia in the desert. I think we all intuited it might be a while before we got anything that resembled a similar experience again. Truth was I hadn't really spent much time with any of the women during the program, but between Spain and a looming book tour, as well as mounting unhappiness at home, I was glad for a reason to stay a few more days in the desert thinking about the cosmos and not so much my own personal constellation of life.

While we did, admittedly, begin by geeking out about everything from Teilhard de Chardin to Cosmic Christ to Kahlil Gibran and the Spanish mystics, we soon found that our central theme of dialogue rested in our individual and collective woundedness. Each one of us was mining through the difficult and profound moments of our own pilgrim's journeys in everyday life. Alone, but all of a sudden in a space of togetherness that none of us expected, a sacredness began to be born. In just 72-hours something like a real community was formed, which I lovingly named "wild women, wild horses," after the desert horses that ran wild. There is something immensely powerful about feeling another person's heart open in front of you, laid bare and completely raw. It feels more alive than almost anything else. There is something ancient about circles of shared suffering and naked truth—that moves throughout eternity, in different languages, always translating into each living moment as the most real thing ever created.

It also seemed no small irony that we were this collective of mystic women in the desert sharing in deep and sacred ways. Something ancestral filled the space. Desert women, sharing our souls and our lives and our pains with each other made me envision the brown and black desert mystics that subverted the early Christian church's alignment with empire to live an alternative way. In our own desert space, we shared the things we hadn't yet spoken into our lives at home: the deep hurt of marriages ending, sexual traumas never spoken out loud to anyone, shame and guilt and hopelessness in life circumstances that felt beyond our control.

In deep grief at the letting go we ended the time together, and I left not knowing if this would be one of those momentary karass moments or something more. Then, something miraculous grew. What was a sacred desert circle became virtualized as we created a Facebook chat group—endearingly named "wild women, wild horses." It seemed we felt called to continue to share the journeys we were walking—somehow it felt lonelier to not have each other as mirrors. None of us knew but opening the door to begin to speak our truth out loud led to a year of unraveling of these truths. Over the next year immense pain and deep healing unfolded from the marriages that had ended, the sexual assaults which were faced and brought into the light, and we were put into life circumstances I don't know if any one of us thought we could have gotten through during those late summer days in the desert. However, we kept returning to each other through each milestone of the journey, each landmark we spoke out loud to each other, even if to no one else in our lives and a deep form of alone-together bonding, unbounded by distance or time apart, formed us into community. There was pain. There was suffering. There were moments of deep solitude as we walked forward through our next year, but there never felt like full loneliness—because we had each other. They became the travelers on my road in a way I never could have expected or would have imagined. Although that season of intimate karass closed in the years following, in some ways these women are a lasting part of my alone-together community and are woven into the karass of my lifeline.

THE PRACTICE: Revealing Your Own Alone-Together Journey

The practice for this chapter calls you to consider your own story. What is the current journey you are on, and what are you walking through that is your own solitary suffering or struggle in this moment? Write that story.

Take your time. There is no rush to write it all in one sitting or to even know exactly what it is in this moment. Sometimes we have to source out the story we are living right now beginning with the present moment. You can ask yourself what is going on in your life today, this week, this month that stands out to you. Is that connected to a larger difficulty, struggle, issue or just life event or experience that you have been moving through over a longer period of time? How would you describe this path you are on right now and what difficulties lie along this particular road?

Then begin to identify who is in your community of support and trust in this present moment of life.

It can be a single person, a group or community of people, or a wider network of people you feel a part of in some way. Who walks beside you on your own journey? Who walks beside you in this moment of your journey that might be new, different or unique versus other parts of your life? Are there unexpected people or communities who have shown up? Are there people or communities who have had to fall away in this time or for this season? Is some of that change or loss temporary for this moment or has some of that change been more permanent and a result of how this current journey is changing you and your life as a whole?

Plan to select a community who you share this time and part of your life journey with in this next part of your practice.

This can be a local community or a community at a distance. In this age where virtual and distant communities can be as potent as local ones, this might be a group of people you meet with in-person or it might be a shared practice you do via virtual technology like Skype or Google Chat.

Everyone in this community is guided to create a shared practice to move through together—whether it is a hike, a marathon, a day retreat, or an adventurous activity.

If you are at a distance this might include taking the alone-together metaphor into a more diverse landscape—where you select a shared day/time to do a practice in your own context but alone-together.

Once you have done the shared practice—either together or in a distanced version of alone-together—find a time to utilize virtual technology like Skype of Google Chat to come together.

During this time share whatever each person is comfortable sharing from your written story/reflection for the current journey you are on (you invite each person in your community and tribe to write this before you get together for this ritual). Light a candle for every story shared to represent light sharing space together even if it is not the same flame. If it is cathartic for each person they can choose what they want to do with their story. Some may want to keep it but if it feels helpful to burn the story each person can do so in the fire of their own candle's flame. The shared practice can be closed with some kind of reading, prayer, poem or song selected by a member of the tribe or community or selected together prior to the shared practice.

CHAPTER 4

Just Keep Walking

ON CAMINO: SCORCHED EARTH

CAMINO IS A bitch on your body. It ravages parts of yourself you didn't even knew existed—discrete muscle groups, worn down parts of skin on the inner regions of your toes, and pretty much anywhere the sun has access to becomes scorched and leathered with increasing intensity each day. I had always been at war with my body, since I was younger when pain began to creep into my muscles bit by bit. There was this unspoken battle fought deep within me—mind over matter in the most literal and intra-personal way. It was me against me and somehow, I could never win. Over time, this unspoken battle took a serious toll on my relationship with my physical self. I began to resent it and rage at it, punish it and shun it, in ways that I didn't even realize were so volatile and abusive. Something bizarre happened through the course of my Camino. For the first time, there was something me (the disembodied cognitive part of me) and my body were working towards and against together—and there was a reparative union that began to happen as we labored in unison.

I had known coming on the pilgrimage that it would be, possibly, my last opportunity to attempt something like it, since the previous few years my multitude of chronic and invisible illnesses were beginning to take a toll on my quality of life and mobility. I had this understanding that it was a now or never situation when it came to the prospect of me hiking for days on end, for even the minimum Camino terrain of 100-kilometers (which of course, as we know, is in point of fact 114-kilometers). What I *had* expected was needing to fight against my body to get where I needed to go. I didn't expect the reverse to happen. I had never planned to find love and respect for the very thing I had spent a lifetime coming to hate as much as one can hate a part of their own self. I also knew that I wanted to walk Camino nearly as long as pain had existed in my body.

I learned about Camino when I was fifteen-years-old and ever since then I knew it was something I was drawn to do. As an enneagram four and a con-summate dreamer I was drawn to Camino through an inevitable lust for the romance of Spanish countryside and the equal adventure of an ancient pil-grimage. Twenty years I had waited for this journey. My body and I came to an agreement of going for a sort of last hurrah of what was physically possible for me. We began grudgingly, in opposition to one another, but as the kilometers passed, a merging re-emerged, where my body and I became symbiotic rather than oppositional forces.

The second half of my Camino, in particular, taught me the most about what my body *was* could do. I had more than twenty years of my lifetime of increased limitation in which both my body and the medical professionals (talking about my body) spent energy convincing me of what my body *wasn't* capable of doing. Endometriosis and my gynecologist told my body it was infertile and pain-filled, a useless set of organs built for one purpose which it was incapable of fulfilling. Fibromyalgia and my rheumatologist told my body it couldn't even properly get out bed in the morning without stiffness and muscles freezing. It told me that on any given day, from head to toe, I would feel like I was run over and given a virulent strain of the flu to the point that it would hurt to move anything. Chronic rhinitis, costochondritis, migraines and my allergist would tell me that my immune system response to even to everything around me would inevitably lead to daily headaches from first thing in the morning and given any stressor would likely bee-line me directly to sinus infections, do not pass go, do not stop at a cold. It would also tell me that I could have breathing incapacitated at any given moment. Everything about my medical record, my doctor teams, and the physical evidence of my body itself would tell me that I could not walk Camino. All evidence would say that I had passed the mark of no return. It had also medicalized my body to such a point that my physical form itself felt like a disease that nothing could quite cure me of, no matter how much medication I was on.

I was almost certain Camino would break us—the disembodied and embodied me, myself and I. I also was committed to attempting to manifest my pilgrimage if there was any chance I could make it through and knowing if it weren't too late already it would be by the next time I had the time capacity to get to Spain.

As the days of Camino passed by something strange and unexpected happened with my body and me. We began to listen to each other. There was no internal battle raging between my cognitive willpower and my body's ability. There was understanding of what was possible and pushing of boundaries only when the whole system of self was on board. When my body said rest—we'd rest. When my body said go—we went. When I asked for us to try for just another kilometer to get to the town we needed to for that day my body agreed to try and so we tried for as long as we could.

It was a deeply empowering and honoring merging of this body I carried—and that carried me—as we made the choice every day to make our way over one hill after the next, looking back after a day's journey to see just how far we had been able to come. Since the walk had become less about who I was walking with, I, and the we inside of me, became the companionship and conversation partner for the journey. And as the road got harder, we needed the intra-personal communication to get through it. Each step was equal to a hillside worth of walking in terms of the internal motivation it took to keep moving forward. Everything hurt, but by that point was as universal to my lived experience as waking up every day. For once, we were walking through the pain together, like an embrace of what was, rather than a revulsion of the uncontrollable other. The pain just was, and would be, and so we walked into it, rather than in spite of it.

The third day I remember very well—it was by far the longest, stretching 22-kilometers between starting and ending points. I did not know the actual distance when I started the day, because at the equivalent of nearly 13.7-miles I would have said a big hell no at breakfast. I also probably would have hopped into one of the taxis which smartly marketed with signs and phone numbers along the walls throughout Camino—waiting to pick up the business of the walkers that fell away from the walk on particularly hard days.

The sun was at its hottest of the days so far and the hills to climb seemed unending—like a nonstop rollercoaster of ups and downs, if rollercoasters moved at the speed of tortoise under the gaze of an undeterred, ever-encroaching sun. Yes, I was the tortoise. There was one point, about two-thirds of the way through the grueling day, after I had stopped an innumerable number of times to let my swollen, bleeding feet rest and released my heavy knee caps from the constant pressure of my backpack, when I began to consider the insanity of this specific proposition.

What was I doing?

Walking through a five-day expanse of Spanish countryside was an absurd idea even under the best of bodily circumstance. I did not have the best of bodily circumstances. Me, the one with all the aches, and pains, the always broken or sprained something. Me, the one with more illnesses and doctors than I could count on two hands. Jose Lado's words and visions of his air-conditioned car danced through my head. Daydreams of his Halloween-style suggestion of trick-or-treating from stamp stop to stamp spot in said air-conditioned car began to permeate my overactive imagination.

What the actual crap was I thinking?

Walking for five days all of a sudden seemed like the least ideal use of my summer vacation time. My internal negotiator came online in full force and began reasoning me out of forward motion.

"I mean," said the voice, in a smooth serpentine voice wooing my brain, "in truth, my end goal is Ávila, so what harm would it be, at this point of physical degradation, to just hop on over to Santiago and sip some Albariño in a lovely hotel until Thursday, when my train could take me to my final destination?"

"I know," I thought as a compromise of sorts between the serpent, my thinking brain and my body. "I should really consult Teresa on this one. If she doesn't respond, I will take that as an affirmation of my new life plan."

"So, here's the thing," I started in my clever, clever way, addressing my pilgrimage patroness, Teresa of Ávila, like I had come to do when I got in a bind or, in this case, I needed some pilgrimage feedback.

"I am really feeling like this pilgrimage ends in Ávila, where we will have our time together in the city of your origin and the city of my naming, so I really don't think I need to finish out this whole walking thing. If you agree, no need to do anything. If you don't just give me some sign and inspiration that I should keep walking."

No sooner had my vague, easy-out clause request been channeled when out from a side alley that I hadn't even seen, came a nun dressed in full garb, rosary in hand, and Teva sandals on foot swiftly charging past me with the purpose of a champ—heading up the never-ending incline ahead of me.

"Seriously?!"

I internally squealed upwards, as I took in the sight of the most literal sign a nun could send to an earthly counterpart on a pilgrim's trail like this.

With a huff, well more likely a few, I thrust my pack back on my scarred and aching back, and continued upwards for what felt like another hour—and was likely as long. Halfway up and still no end in sight, the sun brighter than ever, and my forceful impetus of the nun sighting waning in terms of motivation I decided to do a follow-up call.

"Ok, so here's the thing. I know there was that whole nun appearing in the road bit—but, maybe that wasn't you, maybe that was just your average Camino coincidence. So, what I propose is this, if you really think I need to finish this thing out—keep on climbing and all—just send me one more signal to confirm the first and confirm my need to move forward. Cool?"

Again, as if in both defiance and mockery of my need for a follow-up check in to the mystical hotline, as I paused there, panting heavily and teetering on the edge of the hill, from behind me there was a second charge. This time it was three nuns, in full habits, clutching rosaries, and, of course (they must have been from the same group), sporting Tevas:

"Alright, alright, alright. Damn it! I get it," I said grudgingly into my head and into the ether of timeless connection and conversation.

From that point forward, on that longest day of the walk, I moved into some hypnotic state somewhere between fortitude and delirium. My body and I had agreed, after the second sign and the obvious forward calling, that we would just do it. We decided that we *could* do it. Soon after the second sighting the never-ending incline leveled out—that constant reminder that I had found throughout my life, that right beyond the threshold of pain you think you cannot bear is the release. It wasn't easy and it wasn't short from that point forward, but the hills were never as long or as steep as that precipice of giving up, and the hour of my habited reinforcements.

The last stretch of that day was treacherous for a different reason. I found myself with a sparse number of fellow travelers as it was edging towards sunset and all the smart and fast (or folks with at least one of those qualities) travelers had started early and arrived at their destination. In addition to that, the last section of the walk was confusing, with multiple intersections unmarked with the tell-tale golden shells or yellow arrows that beckon peregrinos forward. I was walking through tall grasses in nearly abandoned countryside paths, through four-way intersections, with only a little map and a GPS on my phone with a waning signal. I wasn't sure at this point if my destination albergue (set in a small side-road away from any major town) was five or fifteen-kilometers but I did remember from the morning's planning session with Marisol that it would be the last one for a very long while.

At one point, when I was near desperation, I passed a little dilapidated farm-house and a woman came walking down the path with a bundle on her back.

She stopped and paused in front of me then said (in Spanish), "Ah, you are a very pretty brown girl."

To which, at this point not sure if she was some fairytale story mirage or real, I said, "Um, thank you."

I am still not certain if this was a compliment or a slight—but I was too tired to even consider the full extent of the strange encounter.

As it began to get darker outside, I saw other peregrinos, in pairs or fours, setting up camp beside the road—and this final sign was what made me exceedingly worried. Had I passed the turn off for the albergue? Did these people know we were past the point of return between towns, and I didn't? I didn't have any sleeping gear. I had no backup plan besides walking. I headed down a very remote dirt path just as the sun began to descend and a chilled wind swept past me—making my aching body shudder. I saw a log and a gravel patch that almost looked clear of hard rocks.

"Well," I thought, "if I go another kilometer and there is no albergue, I guess I will just sleep here, on this log."

That was my whole plan. I guess I shouldn't have dropped out of Brownies before they became Girl Scouts. Right as I was about to turn around and claim my patch of dirt in the name of the United States of Teresa(s) I saw the dirt path become a paved road, and I could make out the top of a roof about a block's distance away. Directly in front of me were a couple of picnic tables and benches on a patch of grass—just a little park in the middle of nowhere on the edge of the Camino trail. Knowing that the albergue was only a block further away my body officially gave out. I spent about ten minutes laid flat on the top of a picnic table before I finally submitted to strapping myself into the backpack prison one more time and stumbling into the albergue—where, to my great gratitude and unending joy, Marisol sat waiting for me with a beautiful bottle of Albariño wine and a delicious bocadillo (sandwich).

I could not believe we had made it—me, my body, and Teresa. One day closer to Santiago. One day closer to Ávila. More than that though, that day taught me what my body was capable of—and it healed an emotional wound between my internal self and my physical self I hadn't realized was so in need of repair. I was physically weaker and more depleted than I had been in a long time—in fact I had to rest my body for a good portion of the next day—but I did it with appreciation of and gratitude towards the body that had gotten me so far. Previously, I would care for my body grudgingly and even the care seemed to do more violence than good as it was still a war I was fighting. I felt no shame for taking much of that next day to rest and felt no failure at having to be gentler with my body after it had given so much. It was the beginning of a different kind of relationship between me, myself and my body—in a way that I have to remind, regenerate and restore time and again, like with any relationship to keep it healthy.

FLASHBACK: MYSTIC PAIN COACH

Since I was thirteen, when I had my first period (yes, I'm a girl and I am saying period, which I know alerts the menfolk to run for cover), I have been in ever-increasing amounts of pain. If I didn't think I had a connectedness to the mystics from the origin of my naming, then I would have been alerted by my lifelong lineage of pain—something that carried throughout the lives of not just Teresa of Ávila, but a number of other mystics throughout time. Sometimes that knowledge of connectedness was the only thing that kept me sane through the pain. That first set of pains which came from that biological signal of "womanhood" at twelve, I would discover over ten years later was the early flares of endometriosis. Although, since it is a women's issue related to pain, which the medical community often underplays, the average time from onset of symptoms to diagnosis is a disgusting decade. One decade for a woman to be believed that her pain is real, and yes, really that bad.

When I finally found a surgeon in my mid-twenties who was willing to perform the laparoscopic surgery to internally diagnose the condition, I had already become an expert on the condition and self-diagnosed as best as I could, before seeking out a provider willing to perform the procedure. It also took four different providers to find one who would even engage the possibility and was willing to do the laparoscopic surgery which is the only certain method of diagnosis. When we discussed his findings after the procedure, me still heavily medicated and in immense pain, he said with shock, "Well, look at that! It's not only endometriosis but Stage 3."

For a frame of reference—there are only four stages and the fourth leads to such medical interventions as colostomy bags, because the endometriosis begins to deteriorate not just the surrounding organ linings but perforates right through things like bladder and bowel. In situations such as these a simple "I told you so" just doesn't quite suffice. For this condition I had four surgeries over just as many years—some to assist in prevention of further pain, the last two to also assist in my ability to get pregnant—which never came to fruition.

The truth is—after about two decades of the illness I had gotten used to the issues, and the various medical ailments that extended out from it. Apparently, with autoimmune-related conditions like Endo (yes, we're on a nickname basis) there is a greater likelihood a person will have or develop a cluster of other issues which are somehow, although no one knows exactly how, inter-connected. I checked a few off the list over the years but none was quite as devastating as when Fibromyalgia came to town. It probably had peeked its head in for a number of years but since my Endometriosis pain was so intense and so constant, I didn't even notice this new guest at the dinner table. Not until Christmas of 2012, right after I turned thirty-two. I remember exactly how it happened and exactly how it felt. My sister was coming that week for her annual Christmas holiday in Florida and I wanted, for whatever bizarre inclination of mine, thoroughly scrub the grout in my home's the tile floors. I decide to bleach out the grout, which I knew would be a day-long endeavor, and so I got my bucket, my bleach concoction, and my toothbrush and settled, somewhat uncomfortably, on my hands and knees to begin the process. About eight hours later I peeled myself off the floor, the job unfinished but my body definitely done. I had this increasing pain in my knees that had started to surge down to my toes about half way through the day and was now pulsing the length of my body—shooting upwards through my abdomen into my chest, my arms, and my fingertips. All I can say is it felt like the equivalent of the worst period cramps I had ever felt—if you could extend that pain to every inch of your body. I didn't quite know what was going on, but I had my heat-ing pad, as always, on standby and so I curled into bed with the heating pad on blast, assuming it would subside by the next day.

The next day extended into the next week and the next month and nothing had changed. It was like the pain I had always felt in my gut had been cranked up on its highest volume and pumped to every muscle and nerve of my body—almost like when you get the fever aches with a really bad flu, but never expiring, never tiring. What I began to realize as the days ticked by and noth-ing changed, using myself as my own medical case study yet again, was that the most intense and overwhelming part, the part that drove you so mad you thought you might lose your entire sanity wasn't the extent or intensity of the pain. It was the duration. Pain, I knew, but pain that never ended—with no landmark on a calendar or in a medical journal to tell me when it would cease, was maddening. And I mean maddening in the most literal sense. It made me feel like I was losing my mind. I couldn't think. I couldn't focus. The pain became the primary thought in my mind, the primary focus of my being—always drawing attention back to it. When forgotten, even for a moment, its ferociousness and its total unwavering presence would force all attention in my beingness back to it as the center of my world.

By the second month I was starting to fray at the edges, and, much like the endo-metriosis, none of the doctors I went to knew what it was or could even validate its existence. At this point, I didn't even have a name for this adversary that was taking over my body and my life, one wretched day at a time. I was listening to meditation CDs, attempting to do yogic breathing practices, anything that could offer me a few moments of rest away from this monster without a name.

Around that time, I had also begun leading a contemplative practice group at the local Episcopal Church I was attending, and I had pile of resource books sitting in my car. One of them was *Mi Vida* or *My Life* which is an autobi-ographical work (my particular copy was translated by the lyrically potent Mirabai Starr) of Teresa of Ávila telling the story of her life, her mystical expe-riences, and her work. I had carried it around for months, pulling it out only to flip to a page and extract a quote for the group, but never reading the book.

In her first visceral presence in my life—although her writing had inspired me for years at this point—Teresa showed up at my edge of nowhere, in that desperation that, I guess, a mystic can see from far away and across time like a hazard sign.

She came booming in, as I would learn over time, was her way, unexpected and none-so-subtle. I was sitting in my car, in my driveway, car idling and body just attempting to be inspired enough to move. Something which had become an immense labor by this point. Teresa's disembodied voice, not quite inside me and not quite external, shouted in a way I almost jolted in the driver's seat.

"Get the fuck up and go get my book. Get it out of the passenger seat of your car. Right. Now. I know you haven't read a word. Don't try to pretend otherwise. Pick it up and read it from the first page. I mean the *very* first page!"

I want to be really clear here. My mystical disclaimer regarding my conversations with Teresa and anything you might have read, known, or heard about the historic person that is Teresa is as follows. I am not saying she would have dropped the f-bomb to anyone else or that she ever has in her tenure on earth and beyond. All I can say is she knows me, and she knew it was the one way to get me up off my ass. As far as I can tell, in all encounters of the divine kind that I have had, your sacred companions come to you with an energy of their own making (the sassy boldness is all her) and in a vernacular you can hear. Hence, the f-bomb, which plays a dominant in my divine dialogues. Now that we have cleared that up, so you don't hyperventilate over my sacrilegious mystical conversations, let's move on, shall we?

I did as she demanded. Mostly, if I am honest, because she was so insistent, and a little bit of a cosmic bully. But what I needed in that moment was exactly a cosmic bully, or as I would later term this kind of support, "motivational yelling." I do really well with a little motivational yelling in my life.

I opened up, to the very first page, and began to read. The foreword was by a woman named Tessa Bielecki, and the translation by Mirabai Starr—both women equally beloved by and loving of Teresa of Ávila, both women I would come to read and read again, their works and words moving through me like the divine rhythm and cadence of Teresa herself. Both women would later become women I would be graced to know and love, hug and be held by in person and through letters to this day. Teresa sent them to me, I am sure, but she began with this push—not just towards them but towards what they wrote. When I read from the very first page, as instructed, in *Mi Vida* I saw the story of Teresa's life laid out, as written by them and her. I saw so much of myself in the pages in ways I had never quite seen. It was so raw and real. When I had previously read her book on spiritual evolution of the soul, *Interior Castle*, it was much more of an instructional manual on spiritual journey. In *Vida* I saw her up close and so vivid, it was like she was not just in front of me yelling and such, but inside of me in a way that comforted me beyond my pain and into it. Most specifically, I saw the history I had never known, first told about her and then in her own words, of her years of agonizing physical pain, undiagnosable by doctors, surrounded by a series of mystical experiences which carried her through the pain and out the other side, over and over again. She was in some manner of pain throughout her whole life, although the most excruciating period did finally pass. Her calling me to read this was like a love letter of hope—knowing both that the pain would be part of my story, and that the worst of it would pass. It gave me the hope of a future that would be beyond the inclining torment of pain that seems never-ending. It reminded me that pain is like a bell graph, with a peak point and a reprieve just past the point you think you cannot bear.

This is not the fullness of this story of pain and release—there would be months more of the excruciating pain, leading to an expansion with breathlessness, an increase in one of my cluster of autoimmune issues leading to asthmatic symptoms, through Lent and into, of all things, Easter Sunday. I spent the day before Easter in an emergency room, following a night of powerful visions and deep presence of the divine. From there I was sent to the Cleveland Clinic where I received the diagnosis of the acute asthma related to seasonal sinus issues and, finally, the diagnosis of my fibromyalgia. It wasn't perfect after that—but I was over a seemingly unbearable, never-ending hill. Mentally, emotionally, and spiritually, however—just like on that incline in Spain—I never would have made it over without Teresa in my face, making sure (in no uncertain terms, and with some motivational yelling) I knew that I could.

FLASH-FORWARD: SITTING WITH THE DIVINE

What I have learned since Camino is the power of mystical companionship and spiritual patronage. After my early experiences of divine presence, both with Teresa and with the wholeness of the divine that I call God, I didn't know what to do with them. I knew they were meant to serve a purpose, not just for me, but outward and beyond me—not in some egotistical way that was about me or the "specialness" of me, but like they were a gift that was meant to be shared. I also didn't know how to do that with maturity and wisdom. After the immense series of experiences I went through, and months following delving into intense contemplative practice, beginning in that December in 2012 and continuing forward to the hilltop in Spain, I sought guidance about what to say and how to say it. The immensity and the power of it made me want to shout it out on blast—megaphone style—with the enthusiasm of a small child with a new toy. That was probably ill-advised, as I was told from my spiritual support at the time—a lovely Cenacle sister (of the Therese of Lisieux lineage) who lived in the local Cenacle house in Lake Worth, Florida.

She said, "You need to sit with it for a while, give it time for the newness of it to fade. You will know how and when to share it, if you give it time."

This was both the best advice and the hardest because I am terrible with patience. Instant gratification is my drug—I want it now, if not sooner. The truth was I needed years to sit with this experience and each and every experience of divine companionship I have been offered to know how to share it in a way that wasn't a kid with a toy and a megaphone. However, as I have grown in my spirituality, and time has given me the ability to see these visitations in a longer history of growing and deepening relationship, it has offered me the ability to see them that way. Not as some new toy, or one-time jolt of mystic unity, but rather small pieces of a growing story of myself in relationship with the divine and those that connect me more deeply with that sacredness, speaking to me in the heart of my heart—like Teresa.

Out of this I can now share this story, here and in talks, in retreats and in my own spiritual companionship with others, as it feels necessary and as it serves the other, on their journey and their deepening relationship with the divine. In the course of writing this book, as I reflected back on the various ways I have been touched by grace and the beautiful experience of that which is most intimately myself and stretches way beyond me, I spent a long time reflecting on necessity. In this place, in this moment, in this writing, these words feel like they serve something greater than me—and in that way they feel necessary, not because of me, or because it is my story, but in spite of it. The evolution of my understanding of this divine relationship and my own relationship to these experiences has been as essential and profound as having them. I offer them up delicately and with love in the hopes that they spark a flame of their inherent truth in your own mystic heart. We all have one—sometimes we just need the fires stoked to remember and reclaim it. In doing so, it becomes clear that nothing in our life is all uphill and we can push through far more pain than we ever thought possible with our own remembrance of our connection to the divine, and our deep connection to the immense power and resilience in ourselves.

THE PRACTICE: A Hill to Climb

The practice for this chapter is to consider a hill you thought you couldn't get over and remember how you got through it. Or, if you are struggling through something in this moment that seems insurmountable consider why it feels that way?

What is the fear that holds you back from moving through the pain or fear or difficulty that seems too great? What has allowed you to move through pain or fear like that in the past? What has stopped you from even trying?

Consider creating a timeline of your life with hills and flat land—when were you able to get over the hills and what were the ones you didn't?

Write them out in a timeline of hills and flatlands (the hard parts and what came after). See the patterns or themes of what kind of things you have moved through and climbed over and what kinds of things you have avoided and gone around.

Take some time over the next week or few weeks to think about the hills you avoided or are avoiding right now.

Begin to visualize what it would look like to push through and over the hill. Think about what it would feel like, what the barriers are, and visualize yourself moving through them. What is your foreseen outcome? What steps can you take to begin to walk upward—knowing that the hill cannot and will not last forever.

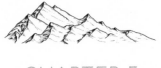

CHAPTER 5

The Last Yellow Mile

ON CAMINO: WALKING IN THE DARK

WE BEGAN WALKING on the last day before dawn in an effort to make sure we got to Santiago by late afternoon. Marisol and I were walking together again. Even in alone-together pilgrimages you get those moments that bookmark the journey with the ones you love the most. I was feeling more equipped to keep up as I had given my body rest for much of day four. As part of honoring of my new embodied relationship I had decided to not push myself during day four. Previously, I would have forced my body, as a masochistic punishment for its inability to meet the body goals of others. Instead I let it get what it needed for a few hours after a long week's walk and as a result I was feeling almost fully restored by the pre-dawn hours of day five.

I was feeling the gravitational pull of Santiago—only a day's walk away. We moved through the quiet town streets with nothing but the steady beat of footsteps, having been joined by a few other folks we had met along the way who were also hoping to get to Santiago by the afternoon. I couldn't help but think back to the previous afternoon and the rule-obsessed albergue captain from the strangest, most regulated night's stay we'd had during the whole trip. I giggled out loud thinking about us tiptoeing around in the dark just moments before to find our socks and poles and clothes, trying our hardest not to break any of the rules plastered in paper signs all over the albergue.

"No shoes here!"

"Walking sticks only in this bin!"

"No noise after 10 p.m. or before 5 a.m.!"

Luckily there had been no rules about putting on socks or dressing before dawn, so I felt assured our ungracious host wouldn't pop his head around the corner and begin shouting as he had at every person at check in.

Walking through the town with the sky so dim we could only see due to the street lamps, following the yellow shells that marked the way out of town and back on the Camino trail, I felt so peaceful. It was like a walking meditation. There had been periods throughout the walk which had felt like this—with the only the beat of feet and the smell of dew on trees. During the day it was harder to drown out all the superfluous noise of conversation, which started to feel intrusive when you were reaching into those deep internal places that come from the rhythm and drum beat of your own footsteps over hours and days. On this early morning, the stillness made for a clear uninterrupted meditation of feet and walking sticks with thumps and clicks and backpack rustling as the primary noise moving us forward. Passing an inn visible from the main road I glanced over and then did a double take, seeing my first horseback Camino trekkers mounting their horses on the cobble stone under an old street lamp light. I felt momentarily transported back in time.

When we reached the forest at the entrance to the final leg of the Camino walk it was so dark we all needed to turn on our headlamps to see and a newly made Camino friend named Sasha from Germany who Marisol had met on day two of the walk said, "This feels like *Blair Witch*."

Of course, I instantly scared myself, something I had the special for ever since I was a child. For the next ten minutes as we walked with nothing but head-lamps in between dense fir trees I twitched at every sound behind me, certain I had somehow been transported into a *Blair Witch* meets *Hostel* film premise, occasionally laughing at myself in an echoing cackle through the trees, making the setting for something wicked no less authentic. As light began to creep through the trees and the forest path made way for a dusty field trail which would take us a good portion of the way to Santiago, I was able to shake off my horror film script and get back into the Camino-zone. Every few minutes the sun shone brighter and the path got more crowded.

This was the last push for us all and everyone was making their way towards Santiago with their own feelings in their hearts and gut about the prospect. Bellies were full of nerves, anxiety, excitement, and anticipation. It was a swirl of a variety of emotions. The one very potent thing about the last day's walk to a pilgrim destination is that you realize this is what you have been walking towards, in this Oz-like way, but it doesn't necessarily hold the answers of how to get home. Not home as in Kansas, the physical place you came from, but the home your heart is seeking. What most often carries people on Camino in the first place is the pursuit of that which is missing, and the needing to let go or find a death to find the new beginning. The Camino may give you time to think, to process, to surmount with your physical body what you want to with your embodied life, but it doesn't do that final work for you. So, as people move their way on the final stretch towards the Emerald City, they realize what they are looking for is harder work than the walk itself. The life you have has to be faced and the things you face wait for you at home.

I felt that strongly with each step closer towards the city I had been walking in the vague direction of for a week. I felt the resonance of that anticipation mixed with a variety of emotions. It was palpable in the reverence on the last day. Even if I hadn't been able to feel it in the air, or if I needed a clue to validate the dense sacredness of the final walk, one of the last spray-painted words I saw warned me. On the interior bricks of the small bridge tunnels along the way and over the days were written messages, over time, to loved ones, to oneself, to the divine. The words I saw on this last day, in bright yellow, in large print, said, "What do I do when there are no more yellow arrows?"

The arrows guide you. They give you a place to go next without having to think about it and without having to make hard choices. Whether you get to Santiago in one week, three weeks, six weeks, three months or more, the city is always waiting, and the arrows always guide the *Way*. The Camino *is* the way. After it is over, you are in the dark again with no certainty of the path forward.

That prospect is frightening. There is something so powerfully comforting about knowing your way, and not much beyond the Camino, in life, offers us that clarity.

I felt my ambivalence as I walked towards Santiago. It was boiling in my belly and held in the fibers of my nerves. I felt my own anticipation of the life I had tried to walk off and had to return to, including the marriage that was mutually unhappy, the work that had become unsatisfying and embroiled in my marriage. I felt the pressure of the life that no longer felt like mine though I walked in it, out of habit, as a shadow of myself. Like a figment of my own imagination. I knew there were hard things ahead. I just didn't yet know how to face them.

But I walked, because for the time being, I had my friend at my side, my walking sticks which had become constant companions and my surrogate legs when walking felt impossible. I had my pack that felt molded to my back, and my boots under which my bloody toes had decided to stop quite minding their condition. For now, at least, I still had yellow arrows to take me where I was going.

As we got closer to the city, Marisol and I began to talk—about the walk, our lives, everything that had brought us here and everything we were carrying home. We talked about the metaphors of the road and the things we never expected. We joked, as people do, on Camino, about those moments of total nervous breakdown. There are moments on Camino when the walking sears through all the barriers you hold in life to keep out your own pain and the rhythm and monotony of just moving with nothing else to do burns up your inhibitions and lets through everything you had been feeling. Often feelings so deeply buried you didn't even know were there, and let's your soul loose. In those moments fellow peregrinos would commiserate that they would find themselves weeping, walking alone, but beside hundreds of strangers. As a result, it just became the expected and common practice in this really liberating way. Marisol and I joked as we walked about how half of everyone's Camino standard greeting of, "Buen Camino!" would regularly come from a fellow pilgrim amid a slur of tears and gasps. The tearful "Buen Camino!" had, over the days, become a new normal.

We knew there would be a final uphill trek, heading walkers above the city before diving down into the center. It was supposed to be a terror to walk, so we kept walking and talking as a method of distraction. At some point, about an hour after we had stopped for lunch, we looked at each other, wondering together when we would reach that final killer peak. During that conversation we got to the top of a hill we had been walking for who knows how many conversations and saw at the overhead view of the city we had heard about which marked the end of the hard part. We looked back in the direction of the hill we had just walked and said, simultaneously, "That was it?"

It was this amazing irony, after all the hard hills, the hard days, the hard walks, the hard feelings, that final hill, the one we thought was going to kill us, didn't. I remembered back to my first book, Mending Broken, and how I wrote of the experience of moving through the pain of trauma to a crescendo which, in childbirth, is called the transition. It is the point where you think you cannot take anymore, and then right over the edge of that pain there is a release. I have found that in every difficult thing I have ever done that it is right when I think I can't go any further that something releases, and the big hill turns out not to be so big at all.

From there we descended into the city down a series of shorter steep and winding hills. This part was actually more difficult for me as I had learned I was great at uphill, but downhills killed my legs. I felt there was probably some emotional metaphor tucked into that physical fact, but for the moment my focus was on getting down that last series of descents, as the city came closer and closer into view. My solution was to walk backwards as the past days had taught me that the pressure on my legs decreased when I walked backwards on descents. So, Marisol and I walked and talked together, smiling and waving "Buen Camino!" to passersby as they took double glances at my strange downhill methodology. Of course, I thought, I would have to walk into the city backwards.

There is nothing like the feeling of walking into the city you have been walking towards for days. There is an immensity and intensity in realizing what your body can do, and for me, what my body and I were able to do together, against all my expectations. Walking towards that final destination, across the final steps that every Camino walker—whether their walk was 100-kilometers or ten times that—had walked to enter this city over centuries was indescribable. It was bigger than me, it was bigger than us, it was walking into and through a sacred part of holy history. Along the way, with the internal processing and the physical immensity, I had lost the memory of the history of this walk somewhere—the Way of St James. Walking into Santiago, with all the knowledge of this pilgrimage and all of the past pilgrims overwhelmed me like a heavy wind. I felt like I was walking into, and was a part of, that holy history.

As we got closer to the main square in front of the Catedral de Santiago, I could hear bagpipes which felt like a trick of my ears. A few blocks further and I could see, under a brick passageway in the last few steps before the square, a man in a kilt playing a bagpipe. It was Celtic and mystical and totally unexpected. I would learn later there was a great crossover of Celtic and Galician history, but in that moment, it was just the right song in the most unexpected place. As I moved past the bagpiper and the surrounding crowd of enchanted listeners, the short passageway gave way to light and open space, into the expansive square and the towering Catedral overhead. Marisol and I made our way to the center of the square where Camino pilgrims were dropping bags and letting their bodies rest in the shadow of the sacred spires above.

We flopped down on the ground, bags and all, and laid on our packs, still attached to our backs. There was an exhaustion that blew over me and into me, like my body was realizing what it had just done, and what it finally had reprieve from doing and felt all its pain and all its tired, all at once. I looked up at the Catedral and prayed—a wordless prayer, because I had no words. I spent them all on the journey. It was just a beckoning for something sacred to imbue me with the strength for what was ahead. I didn't know fully what that would be, how intense the next months and years of my life would be, or how important that prayer said without words would be, but I needed it and so I sent up a call for strength, and a reminder of the strength the Camino showed me I had.

Sitting there on the ground I did realize that I had fulfilled a yearning almost twenty years old, from a 15-year-old girl who was enthralled with the idea of such a journey. Not only that, but I had done it with my body which I had fought against for so many years only to find that we could do more than we imagined when we worked together. I knew there would be many moments of walking in the darkness ahead. There would be more days of uncertainty, of wrong turns, of no more yellow arrows, but I also knew I could do it. Somewhere deep inside I also knew I would need to revisit this moment again and again at the lowest places to remember that was true, but again, I knew I could do it.

That night, after splurging on a hotel room with comfy beds and delectably soft sheets, Marisol and I set out on the town to celebrate. This began with a task we had set forth from the start of our trip—Camino tattoos. For me, tattoos had always been much a sacred experience as praying before spires. I had written out my journeys and pains, landmarks and special moments, in ink on my skin. My body's markings told the story of my life. Elephants in Chiang Mai, Thailand after visiting rescued elephants at the Elephant Nature Park. Calla lilies and orchids woven together, a joining of my grandmother and my favorite flowers, forever intertwined. A tree of life with a gecko and a trinity symbol woven inside the bark to symbolize the beginning of new life when I moved with my (then) new husband from New Jersey to Florida. And the tattoo on my right wrist, that I got with Marisol, on our first pilgrimage together to Los Angeles for our birthdays: every journey is a pilgrimage. That night, at the end of our shared Camino, we set out to complete our circle of tattoos and friendship. I was adding another tattoo on my left wrist which would be the pilgrim's symbol of the Camino shell. She would be getting the same.

We found a local artist and the piece was so simple it took little time to get both of them done. It was far more symbolic than the little blood drawn and the limited pain of their inscription. After mine was finished I looked at my left wrist and then both my wrists side-by-side and I saw the story of not just this journey, but all my journeys woven back and forth in time and in ink between my wrists and in the reminder that *every* journey is a pilgrimage. I had always known from somewhere deep inside, and I carried the shell on the alternate wrist to remind me. I would carry my pilgrimage with me wherever I went and whatever the next step one the road would be. I would walk in darkness, across the precipice of hard hills and easy ones, I would move through the transition of pain that wasn't possible and find that it was—because I was a pilgrim. Because we all are pilgrims. Because the memory of that moment and the message for a lifetime was written on my wrists.

FLASHBACK: LILIES FOR GRANDMA

I never knew my grandmother well in life. She had a stroke in 1982, when I was only two-and-a-half-years old, and after that she was a whisper of herself, although I would argue even the version of her before her stroke was already a whisper of her true self. She had spent her childhood being emotionally tormented and abused by her older sister who took every opportunity for cruelty and made sure my grandmother would grow into a woman who thought little of herself, and believed the world felt the same. My grandfather had always been the grandparent figure of my childhood. After my grandmother had her stroke, he became matriarch and patriarch, forgoing traditional standards out of necessity and doing everything from cooking and cleaning to lovingly bathing my grandmother, taking her to the bathroom, and making sure she was always as comfortable as possible. He became my foreground, and the ghost of this woman I could barely see became just the backdrop to my loving granddaughter story with him. I knew there was a person in there, underneath the brokenness of a cruel childhood and the frustration of a half invisible body. I remember as a girl trying to imagine what it would be like to not have use of half my limbs, prying into the imagination of my mind to try and understand her. I would sit in my attic bedroom and "practice" making the left side of my body being limp. I would mime what I saw her do when she had to move her own arm from one place to another and imagine what that kind of half-life would feel like. That actually became a strange practice that carried into adulthood. Periodically, when I would try to feel close to her, to who I thought she might be, I would hold my arm and move it, like a limp doll, to get inside something and someone I couldn't quite touch.

When I was fifteen and angry at the world, angry at the entity that I called God, and in the process of abdicating my Christianity by boxing up every sacred memorabilia I had and throwing it out the skylight window, my mother attempted a sort of spiritual intervention. She told me a story she hadn't told anyone else before about my grandmother. I was angry that God hadn't ever shown God-self to me and I was sick of the hypocritical humans I saw within the institution that stood in God's stead. I figured if I didn't have connection to the source, and the conduits were poor versions of misinformed lackies, that there was really no reason for me to stick around for the sham of it all. My mother thought this story would coax me back to the possibility and the accessibility of the sacred.

She said, beginning in the mid-late 1960's that my grandmother began to have visions. She had been a very devout woman, looking to God for the nurturing that the world hadn't always offered her, and feeling a deep devotion to Mary. She went to church every Sunday and found great comfort in her morning rosaries, said kneeling by her bedside. One morning, during her rosaries, she had a vision of Christ on the cross, appearing to her as just a flicker. It was so dim she wasn't sure it had even happened. Over time the visions persisted, increasing in their vividness and with them came sweeping sensations of warmth and love. As they grew in intensity my grandmother became full of fear. She was uncertain what they meant, why they were there, why they came to her, and what they expected of her. In my belief, retrospectively, I think her deep insecurity of her own worth brought fear with those expressions of God's love. Because she had such a deep feeling of unworthiness it was hard for her to fathom herself being someone who would be shown such love from the one entity she had spent her life devoted to. Then of course that is exactly why. Because of her love.

One of her later visions was the full image of Mary, appearing before her as she knelt, and surrounded at her feet were a seemingly endless overflow of roses. In the way that visions offer up a wordless understanding, after a moment she realized that each rose was for each rosary she had prayed in devotion to Mary. It was the gift returned. Her final experience of the divine was just before her stroke and came, again, as she was kneeling and praying the rosary. She was moving through the beads, and moving through the mysteries (sorrowful mystery, joyful mystery) and as she progressed, she began to feel an overwhelming sensation of warmth and love, and the physical sensation of being hugged.

She asked, "Who is this?"

A voice from inside and all around replied, "I am who am."

She was filled with a surge of love like she had never felt before, an overwhelming abundance of grace and goodness holding her.

A few months after that, on August 15, 1982, also the Feast of the Assumption of Mary, she had her stroke. This was the day in the Catholic Church when the death and rising of Mary to heaven is celebrated. I believe it was her beloved mother Mary, holding her in the earthly death of the life and body my grandmother had, which wouldn't return in her lifetime. Also, I think it was a reminder of something else, beyond the stroke. I think it a symbolic reverence of her own grief and an acknowledgement that her life would be very hard until the day she died. Although she never fully returned to who she was, she never forgot her visions and experiences of God. She would remember and hold them with her till her final ascension from this life in 2005 at age eighty-five. She died asleep in her bed and ascended as had her foremother Mary, from this place to the next.

Of course, as the frustrated, angry and passionately stubborn fifteen-year-old I was, when my mother first told me this story instead of being placated by it, I was jealous. I wanted to know, in my spiteful teen way, why she would get the visions I so desperately wanted. Why could I not manifest God that this woman, who I didn't know, couldn't understand, and seemed so disconnected from beingness, could without even trying? I left Christianity frustrated with religion as I knew it. Although I thought I left the stories behind, and the memory of her experience, I never did. Underneath the seething bile of adolescence rife with my anger at the world, anger at God, anger at my birthmother, anger at my inability to understand myself in a white world in brown skin, there was a flicker of my own self that needed to be fully birthed. That person wasn't ready for my grandmother's story at fifteen, and probably still wasn't fully ready at twenty-five, when my grandmother died.

The night before my grandmother died, she was stable and in the hospital near my parent's house in Summit, New Jersey where I was living as I finished up my latent bachelor's degree in English Literature (Women Studies minor). I had left to go out with friends and half way there I had this feeling I had to turn back. My mother had called and said they were all visiting Grandma that evening (she, my father, my brother and sister) and I suddenly had a feeling I had to turn around. By the time I got back to town it was past visiting hours and before I could prepare to go in the morning at 6:38 a.m. we got the call saying she was gone. I felt grief rush over me in a way I didn't expect. I felt a loss of something I never had—a connection to her. I couldn't get back a lifetime or even a minute of knowing her. I couldn't get back an unsaid "goodbye" and an unspent last night together. I was overwhelmed with the impossible. I cried myself to sleep that night and flickers of the story my mother told me began to creep back in as I wept into my pillow and grieved this woman of great visions who I would never see in full.

I fell off to sleep and into a strange dream. It was a dream that didn't feel like a dream, like none that I had ever had before. I found myself at a picnic ground, or what I would later call the "visitor's room" lined with endless picnic tables. I didn't know anyone I saw around me, but people were arriving with gifts and balloons, engaging in tearful greetings and goodbyes. I knew I was somewhere between places, but I didn't know between what. I found an empty table and sat down and as I did, I saw my Grandma coming towards me, in her wheel-chair, which we both knew she didn't need any more. We also both knew she used because it was how I had known her in life. She came up and I cried, not in actual tears but on the inside.

We began to talk, but there were no words spoken, and there was no definable way to determine time. I don't know, as a result, how long we were there, but I know that in the space we shared, in wordless connection, and unsaid storytell-ing, we told each other everything. She knew everything about me down to the deepest part of my soul. She understood better than anyone ever had my pains, my secrets, my stories, my life. And I learned everything about her, all her truth I had tried to claw at in our shared lifetime but could never manage to see. It was beautiful. We were the greatest truth of ourselves, laid bare before each other. We parted with an ending that felt like a beginning and for me that was the day my relationship with my grandmother began. She was with me when I woke up, not in a conscious way, but in a way where I knew that she would watch me, walk with me and be besides me when I needed her. She would be a patron saint, a friend, and someone like Teresa to me. I never knew her in a shared lifetime, but in eternity we would become intertwined and inseparable.

At the tail end of my onset of fibromyalgia beginning over Christmas of 2012, I had a night of great pain and dark visions which exploded over Lent. During this episode, which lasted, in increasing intensity over a period of 12-hours, my grandmother appeared, came to my side and didn't leave until I was at the doctor's the next morning. Like the champion of my soul, she has come to me always in death, and in my greatest mystic frights, in a way she couldn't have in life. She is always with me and her visions return to me often as I feel a synchronicity of much of our experience across time and lifetimes. The fifteen-year-old me couldn't see the gift of her story, but as I aged I realized that the hearing of that story was a sort of preparation for a life I could not have expected was waiting for me and a mystic journey that was far beyond what my envious spirit yearned for when I once wished for God-magic in my life.

My mother told me as I was writing this book and this story, "Grandma always thought I was connected to what was happening to her, and her visions, but really, it is you."

FLASH-FORWARD: YEAR IN REVIEW

My wedding anniversary was New Year's Eve. A note of suggestion: never make a relational anniversary on a major holiday. Even more so, never make it on New Year's Eve, perhaps the most highly pressured arbitrary holiday in the year. The burden of that day is already too much, needing to symbolize both the end and beginning of an entire year. Add a wedding to that and each year the weight is not just on a year but on a year of marriage with great pressure on its appropriate level of specialness. Going back and remembering every year of my marriage I realized we would attempt to make it special and important to the point of its own destruction. Every year it would end in some explosive argument. The pressures of the day were woven into the fabric of our mutually fiery dispositions created combustions equal to the fireworks dancing above our arguments, playing out the rhythm to our missteps.

When December rolled around in 2015, just one month after my separation had begun, the burden of heading directly from life collapse into a holiday season was excruciating. I was feeling so much, but none of it was particularly festive.

It is amazing, no matter how much I had spent so much of my life abdicating and unwriting the scripts of womanhood, forgoing Emily Post's guide to being a lady, and standing in critique of all religiously-affiliated doctrinal "shame" related to divorce, I still felt shame when the divorce was mine. I realized, although I had almost ended my marriage the year before the actual end had happened, I had stopped going forward because of this internal fear of failure. There was a deep shame I felt weighing down on me, amid the pain and grief. I felt the failure of having to amend "till death do us part" to "irreconcilable differences." It wasn't all me or all on me, but at least half was me. Most marriages don't die without the participation of both parties. You make a life together and you unmake it together, with each day, each fight, each distanced silence of unsaid things and the over-saying of things you can never take back. Marriages are ended by choices and harm, to self and the other. For me, I could look over the rubble of what was and see the shards of our history, covered with dust and demolished into submission, that served as the landmarks of our demise. When you begin a marriage, you say one big "yes," but the ending is a long series of tiny little "nos." Some are so imperceptible you might not even see all of them until you do the post-mortem on the body.

I headed back to New Jersey for my holiday season from my couch-camping temporary housing in Asheville, North Carolina. I felt the foreboding of the impending holidays hanging heavy over my head, most especially New Year's Eve. It waited with a vengeance to take down any semblance of functionality and self-esteem I might have accrued since falling apart in that same house the month before. At the very least I wanted to do better than weeping in front of Crocheted Mary all night. I had a pretty good feeling she was starting to mind.

I immediately opted out of any scenario that would force me into feigned celebration and jubilation and decided the safest place for my heart and soul would be with people, but with the least amount of interaction and, if at all possible, where there were no men folk whatsoever.

Ah, to the nunnery.

Yes, ye ole holiday monastic retreat with the ladies who peppered my life story—nuns. A quick google search led me to the Benedictine Sisters at St. Walburga Monastery and their New Year's retreat which began in the afternoon on New Year's Eve and concluded mid-day on New Year's Day. Walburga was an 8th century nun and abbess who was known after her death in the local tribes and communities as "grain mother" originating from the pagan legends of one who protects the crops. She also became synonymous with a festival, named after her, which gave reverence to the crops and held a witchy sort of significance, similar to Halloween. Grain mother made me think of "corn mother" and the North American indigenous legends of the mother of all, the keeper of the crops, and the matriarch of the land and its people. It felt good to be nestled into this monastery whose founder crossed traditions and histories to mother her ancient world and bridge the divide between spiritual lineages. It also always felt good, like a flicker of a home I once knew, to be in the company of sisters. In truth it would always be a flicker of home from my past with the memory always fresh near the surface of being raised, first, in an orphanage house full of nuns, and my lineage of childless mothers, nurturing me through my hard places.

The retreat was to be mostly in silence, with the opening and closing meals in community and conversation and the rest filled with a monastic rhythm of prayer hours and contemplative practice, sharing space, but carrying it alone-together, through to a midnight closing prayer. I didn't know what I would find in the space of that much silence, but I was also deeply comforted to not have to perform my "alright-ness" for one day. I wanted the freedom of not having to force smiles and feign balance in a life totally off-kilter. The space of silence was like a second home. In long spaces of silence, I had always found companionship of the deepest kind, within myself, within the divine, and for much of my life within the pages of books where words held me like a warm embrace for as long as I would let them. I was hungry for silence and the anonymity of shared space without any expectations of who or how I needed to be.

I enjoyed the time chatting with sisters and retreatants for dinner, but I was so starved for silence I was glad when we made our way to the opening prayer and I could nestle inside into a place most familiar. We would enter the sanctuary for prayer and the hours between was time in our room, our little monastic cells, for writing, reading, reflection and private prayer. As the hours got later, I began to hear the spark of early fireworks crackle in the distance and I was so glad to be nestled behind walls, in the sanctuary of this place, in the silence that penetrated internally while protecting externally. Each hour I fell deeper and deeper into the spell of monastic quiet, nestled in the house of the grain mother, and surrounded by the comfort of sisters. Each period of silent contemplation, in breathing community and silence as we gathered for periodic shared prayer space between independent quiet, sent me deeper into the place inside, and into the heart of holiness. With each breath I felt the nearing of the divine, and I felt the presence of my mothers and matriarchs, the known ones of my grandmother and Teresa, encircling me with the protection of their love and the hopefulness of their resilience, and the new ones of these Benedictine sisters and St. Walburga, the grain mother. The deeper in I went, the more the comfort and love surrounded me. When midnight struck, at the close of the final prayer for the evening, we all turned to each other and proceeded in silent hugs and smiles of gratitude. In the silence the proximity to another grew the intimacy in a way that words could never grasp at so quickly.

I went to bed, turning off the lights, and feeling the relative blackness of the space. The street lights were obscured from my side of the building making even the darkness feel overwhelmed with shadows. Suddenly, the room filled with something that was the opposite of warmth. It was harsh and sharp, and in the glimmer of light seeping through the window, I felt I could see a shadow of some kind. I had felt this sensation only one other time—where the energy became so sinister, I almost couldn't breathe, and I felt something there that I couldn't quite see.

It was the Good Friday before Easter, the year that my fibromyalgia showed up as an unwelcome visitor, to be joined by breathlessness of asthma leading into Easter day. That night I felt like I was going to die as the increasing numbness mingled with acute pain overwhelmed my body and I wondered if I would pass out and never wake up. That was the only other night I had felt something negative consume the space around me—unseen but known to me. It was something in the darkness that was made of shadow and ill-intent. I don't know how matter like that is created, but I know that *only* in the spaces where I have felt the deepest presence of divinity has this visitor come to see me.

I don't know if the energy is born in that moment as an accumulation of the pain or an opposition to the divinity holding space where it normally doesn't live. I don't know if it is energy born of something sinister, coming to overwhelm all that is good and turn that matter into ugliness. I do know, both times I experienced it up until that point, it felt evil. It felt tangible, and it wanted to overcome me. Both times, the accumulation of warmth and light and my circle of saints stood watch between me and the shadow, as watch guards of my soul and keepers of my heart. Both times, even as someone who could scare myself with my own scary story and who would turn all the lights on after a horror movie, I was never afraid of harm. I knew in a way that my singular self, with its machinations of everyday panic and fear never did, that I was protected.

In that room in the monastery I laid in bed past midnight and into the early dawn lingering in that place between—between my watchers and my menacing visitor. I lay in the space where one year ends and another begins. Eventually, as the sun began to rise and light the shadow in the room, the sensation of my visitor began to fade like smoke dissolving little-by-little. The energy that had filled the space was also emblematic of this year in transition. The heaviness and the shadow lingering in my life had not consumed me. And I had champions of my heart and soul who I knew would always watch over me, in this place between places, into always.

THE PRACTICE: Embodied Storytelling

The practice for this chapter is to consider what is indelible in your life—if you were to tell your narrative in ink, on your body, what would it look like?

This practice is one of creative expression and imagination, of remembering and imprinting on us what matters. What most matters to you—what has left its mark on your soul.

Like many of these other practices, this can be done individually or with others—I think this one can be especially fun when done in community.

You can do it one of two ways—depending on how messy you want to get:

1. *The less messy way: Make an outline of your body on large butcher paper, craft store paper, or by putting a series of sheets of paper together.* Then, on that body outline, begin to paint in the stories you want imprinted on you—your indelible memories. Later, you can take a picture and post it somewhere to remind you what really matters. You can also take time to journal or discuss the experience in community. How did it feel? Did it look how you expected it to? What surprised you? What made you feel deeply?

2. *The messy way: Get washable non-toxic paint, safe for the skin, and do the same thing but this time not an outline of your body—this time you paint your story on your actual skin.* You can do this in a bathing suit if you want to get as much workable area as possible or in whatever is most comfortable to you. The process and questions are the same in reviewing the final product. Let it dry and wear it around for a day if you feel daring or wash it off right away, if you like. See how it feels to make your indelible memories visible and alive on your own skin.

CHAPTER 6

Hobbling Towards Holiness

ON CAMINO: THE VERY, VERY BAD THING

AFTER CAMINO ENDED, and after the one night's hotel stay I ended up spending a second night's rest in Casa de Marisol where I was able to do some laundry and repack my bag with everything I had from Camino and the things I had left behind in storage at Marisol's family house while we were on the road. My pack overfilled and ready to go I hopped back into Señor Lado's car for transport to Santiago's city center, where I had two-thirds of a day before my overnight train to Ávila departed. I was so proud of my body and my systemically off-balanced equilibrium, with its propensity to snap, crackle and pop at the sight of any bit of dirt or rock. The fact that I had made it all the way to my walking pilgrim's end without incident felt like much more than a minor miracle. My pack was so heavy from my repacking that I decided to make my way towards the post office where they offered the service of storing travelers' backpacks as they wandered the city. The post office was right off the central circle of cobble stone streets that surrounded the Cathedral where the famous peregrino masses happened daily welcoming the pilgrims who had received their Compostela (certificate of completion) in the previous 24 hours.

I reached the post office and swung off my pack, as I had done dozens of times over the last week, on days filled with much more hard travel than a commute by car into town. At this point it was a process of muscle memory. Swinging my bag up. Swinging my bag down. This time as I swiftly lowered it to the ground, I felt a very bad thing happen somewhere around my kneecap. I am actually a huge expert at the sensation of very bad things happening in my body, and I am usually able to immediately suss out the difference between the very bad thing, the somewhat bad thing, and the only slightly bad thing when it happened at a bodily level. This particular bad thing was, I discerned on first screech of pain shooting through my knee and outward, a very, very bad thing. Days upon days, kilometers on kilometers, all carefully walked for the constant and eminent concern that somehow, I would fall, twist, crackle or pop something unwanted. All those days and all those kilometers I had made it without incident. Then, at the doorstep of the post office of Santiago, on what amounted to a leisurely day of sacred city tourist things, I do the very, very bad thing to my body by taking off my pack.

Did I mention it was at the post office? Humiliating.

Even in that moment I knew how ridiculously humiliating it was to do severe harm to myself doing nothing whatsoever. I could hear the conversations to come, like awkwardness foreshadowed, in my head.

"Oh, no! You injured your knee on Camino. I have heard parts of that can be so treacherous and hard on the body. Where did it happen?"

"Um, well…at the post office."

"At the post office along the Camino?" they would say, hoping there was some much more fascinating or tragic piece to the story I was somehow leaving out.

"No. Not really. After the Camino. The post office in Santiago the day after I finished the Camino."

Then I would hobble away, with a forlorn and sad little slouch to my limp.

Over and over it would happen—that conversation. Pilgrim of the hillsides, walker of the many kilometers, wounded at the post office. I just knew it would feel as ridiculous as it did in that moment every time I had to recount it.

As I sometimes did when a medical thing would happen to me, I figured the best first line of response to an impossible situation was abject denial. I would *not* be wounded at the post office. I had all of Santiago to see, I had my patroness' city of Ávila to get to! I was not going to be deterred by any post office-related injury. This was not what was going to take me out on this particular pilgrimage. No, thank you! I ignored the level of pain, just reprogramming my brain to receive only part of the pain receptors.

The one perk of being chronically ill or injured for the better part of my adult life and having managed terrible and long-term pain was there were a few physiological tricks I had up my own particular chronically inhibited sleeve. I may have been accessing my intentional denial protocols, but I wasn't a fool. I went right from the post office, sans backpack, to La Farmacia. Ah, La Farmacia, my old and dear friend. Outside of hospitals one of the things I could access well and easily on almost any continent was a pharmacy. Luckily, there was one only a block away from the post office. I purchased myself the finest ace bandage a limited amount of money could buy, forced it over my quickly swelling left kneecap, ignoring the warning signals that, you know, a body sends you of acute distress, and made my way about my day. I also made sure to get a hearty supply of naproxen to make sure I was aiding in the pain deflation which would, in turn, help with my denial protocols.

I have noticed that some of the most powerful spiritual experiences are often catalyzed by acute physical pain. There is something about pain, besides its inherent function as warning signals for the body, which makes everything more acute to the senses. That pumping of adrenaline through your system makes you unavoidably aware of your own presence in every moment and makes you really absorb what you are experiencing. In that way it does wonders for the power of the mystical and the sacred mystery. I would not recommend it, and I never do it on purpose, but then I sometimes wonder if that is what all those ancient monastics were trying to do with all those self-flagellation practices. Yes, for all that morbid self-punishment, but also, pain is a hell of a high. I seriously do not recommend it, and I would trade opting out of a lifetime of pain for a lifetime of, well, *not* pain, but it has a weird symbiosis with the full visceral experience of life and of the divine. There I was, in Santiago, where millions of people have trekked towards for centuries, in this acute pain, and although it was terrible it was also a beautiful day.

I had received a thorough dose of medieval Catholic churches along the Camino path with the daily visits to countryside churches where elderly women and men would be seated at rustic tables with stamps and ink awaiting travelers on their journey. Some of those travelers entered the space in reverence and prayer, some in a rush, but all came through the doors, as two stamps a day was a mandatory part of the rite of passage to be a "validated" peregrino on the Way of St. James. That said, there was nothing to that point that matched the awesomeness of La Catedral in Santiago. As I wandered, leaning right and hobbling my way, around the darkened interior of the church I found a long hallway off the main sanctuary lined with intricately carved wood confessionals. There was one for a number of European languages from the nearby countries: French, English, Spanish, Portuguese, German, Italian, Polish. As I walked past the doors, I could hear the faint whispers of secrets being offered up to the divine and the rhythm of the ancient pastime in response, prayers given to the penitents.

Beyond the hall of penance, moving along the exterior walls of the entire church structure, encircling the sanctuary center there was a space filled with the deeply imbedded scent of incense which swung on its daily trapeze at the Pilgrim's Mass. Behind that central altar space were tiny stone caves, many with statues of saints barred inside of the cavern enclosures smelling like dampness, lit by candles and haunted by dancing shadows. A handful of these caves were deeper than the rest and inside there were folding wooden chairs set up in an arc. Each tiny prayer rooms built out of stone, with altars at the front. Each one of the tiny rooms had notices out front listing prayer times, each cavern of prayer, like the confessionals, set for different languages. I arrived at the door marked "English" about ten minutes before the next daily prayer time listed as Centering Prayer. Something about a cavern of rocks, the smell of incense, and a darkened circle of centering prayer made me feel at home and allowed me to settle into the pain mounting in my leg for a little while.

In many ways contemplative practices, like centering prayer, had not only been a root of my own spirituality but they had also become a regimen of response to my lifetime of expanding and deepening cycles of pain. Meditation didn't quell suffering completely, but it dimmed its impact enough for me to breathe.

I sat in the quiet and just breathed—deep inhales and deep exhales, letting the spasms in my leg wash over me, like the rhythm of a drum, like the rhythm of my own heartbeat. Before long a priest entered the room, a white man with a white beard shuffling towards the altar and beginning with a thick Irish accent that seemed befitting this particular cavern of rock and prayer. He opened by passing around a basket with shells—the inherent emblem of the Camino. We held the shells throughout the prayer period, and they were gifted to us to take with us after the session closed. This Irish priest led us into centering prayer with a soft but brisk prayer fizzling off into silence. The space vibrated with the energy of centuries of collective silence so intensely I could almost feel the physical presence of the past like wind whipping by me in every direction. The buzz of that echo filled me up and dimmed out the pain. It held space for something sacred and particular, in a way that I knew I would remember that strange little cave and that moment specifically long after. The prayer completed, we all walked out in silence, with our new shells in hand and our collective prayers buzzing to a boil around us.

As dusk crept in, I made my way back to the post office, collected my bag, weighting my right foot so as to decrease pressure on the left, and with a deep breath I braced myself for the impending pain uptick. I took another deep breath in and I swung my pack on my back. The pain was almost impossible to bear and it likely would have been, had there been any other options. If there was a cot in that moment, right next to me, I imagine I would have flung myself on it, like Tom Hanks in the movie *The Burbs* also shouting, "Take me to the hospital! I'm done!"

However, in lieu of other options it is amazing how quickly the impossible just becomes the necessary. I crept my way towards the train station knowing that soon I would be in Ávila and in my personal mecca of pilgrimage. Soon I would be in Ávila. Soon I would be in Ávila. That was the only mantra that could get me through the searing pain, the throbbing swell, and the deep sense that this was in fact a very, very bad thing.

I wouldn't realize until two weeks later, back in the States and at an orthopedist's office, that my not-so-ignorable mishap had in fact been a *full* ACL tear in my left knee. You know, the kind of injury that athletes get from horrific impact blows on the field of one sport or another. It's the kind of injury they carry you off the field on a stretcher from, because the pain is so bad you can't move. Yeah, that kind. What can I say, I guess I can handle my pain like some people can handle their bourbon. It takes a lot to knock me down and keep me down, especially when sacred cities are on the line.

FLASHBACK: MOSQUITO POX & MAE PERM

It was late summer, I was twenty-seven, and it was the year I finished grad school at New York University. I headed out from New York a few months after graduation for a month in Southeast Asia and on my first solo backpacking trip. I woke up at 5:00 a.m. three days into the trip at a guesthouse in Chiang Mai and realized why mosquito nets where critical in monsoon season in northern Thailand. I had been laying throughout the night on my right side and I woke up in my air-conditioned room without a single opened window to a horrific sight. My entire left side was covered in bright red welts. My *entire* left side, meaning my head, face, arms, torso, and legs were covered in quarter-sized raised red lumps.

I had tossed my malaria pills away two days earlier in Bangkok because they were giving me some killer nightmares. In pre-dawn Chiang Mai, I will now admit without shame, I lost my shit. The sheer size and number of these mosquito boils made me look like something no one wants to see in public. Besides that, my careless forgoing of medicine to prevent the very disease that these Jurassic bites could hold while I traveled alone through the northern tip of a country I didn't know, far from home, did something to distort my adventurous traveler spirit into something more like a whimpering inner monologue. I can get anxious and without a touch down to something that looks like calm I can become like a tornado of anxiety in 3.5 seconds. It makes me the weirdest traveling paradox ever. Not three previous to this Asia trek I had decided without thought to swim in a river full of crocodiles in the Pantanal (jungle) of Brazil. No fear to all fear there I was, the same person, catastrophizing the very worst as I stared in the mirror at my body covered with mosquito bites.

I began to consider a quick flight to Tokyo, forgoing the travels further north into Thailand highlands, and east into Laos, and considered mending my "malaria" in a major metropolitan city surrounded by the reassurance of abundant sushi. As I stood there, heart pounding to the disordered rhythm of my own runaway thoughts, I began to feel the truth of my own fear emerge. Sure, I was a little scared about the prospect of malaria, and somewhat terrified of heading out into the daylight and human interaction looking like something that should be quarantined, but my fear was greater than all that. It was the fear of being alone in the unknown. I was 8,500-miles and 23-hours of plane travel from anything and anyone I knew, and I was there completely alone. It is what I had asked for and what I anticipated in many ways but there is something about being truly alone which you can never fully prepare for it.

It is like learning to walk, all over again, on new terrain, but beyond that, on new feet. I was terrified of the anonymity of my life in this land, a place where no one knew me, no one was with me, and I had this feeling that I could just disappear into my own reflection and no one would even know. I lacked the certitude of the tangible and graspable quality of my own existence in a way that felt both literal and existential. Without the mirroring of another, in the quiet of this early morning, in the northern reaches of Thailand I wasn't sure I was anything at all without the reflection of another.

If a Teresa falls in a forest, does she even make a sound? If she disappears from some malaria attack would anyone even know?

There is something about traveling alone which I didn't realize until that moment, that translates into doing life alone. You have to have a foundation on which to build your existence that isn't externally bound. We need relationship and mirroring (seeing and being seen) as sustenance for our souls. However, to exist in a world where that is never promised and often unstable, we have to find ground to stand on that can be solid regardless of being alone or with another. When we build relationship as the core of our being we foster dependency and even when, in my case, I had thought I had built a foundation of self in my own singlehood and personhood that stood firm without the mirroring of another, I realized that I was still living in the shadow of who I thought I should be, rather than the cosmic truth of who I always was. I wasn't even sure how to claim that, yet, but that morning paranoia revealed the deficit I hadn't been able to see until it wrote itself in large lumps over the length of my body—illuminating fear and illuminating the absence of foundation. The fear was as much a fear of invisibility and a fear of disappearing as anything else.

Then, like a flicker of something more than myself, beckoning me forward, I remembered where I was headed. In many ways I had been drawn all the way to Thailand through three stopovers and twenty-three hours in transit for one particular purpose. I was reminded of this when I recalled there was a bus that was coming to pick me up in just three hours to take me to The Elephant Nature Park nestled deep inside the Mae Taeng Valley north of Chiang Mai. The park was a preserve for rescued elephants, abused and traumatized by the logging and tourism industry. I had become enamored by the story of the park after watching a National Geographic special about its founder Lek and her mission to reform the training of elephants to be a relational and humane process, and to offer traumatized elephants a safe home and family for the rest of their days.

As a sexual trauma survivor and someone who had spent the last 16-months in my accelerated master's program studying and treating Post-Traumatic Stress Disorder, I could think of no better mecca of my work, passion, and life's journey than this place of restoration for both human and animal suffering. The recollection of why I came all the way to Thailand and where I was headed was the only thing that made me forgo my panicked plans to evacuate to Tokyo and to move forward, into the deeper forests, heading towards the elephant sanctuary. Despite a completely engorged and swollen left side of my body, I got on that bus.

The park was like nowhere else. It was set in a valley of grasses alongside a rushing river, surrounded by Thai forest, and in the center there sat a cluster of sleeping huts on stilts, encircling covered feeding and sleeping zones for the elephants which sat in the very middle of the structures. The rescued elephants roamed free throughout the day, each one with their own designated *mahout* (trainer)—there was one trainer for each elephant at the park. The mahouts walked beside the herds but didn't interrupt their natural flow of life. Their primary purpose was to keep the elephants safe and, in their own rehabilitation, learn a new method of training and being in relationship with elephants that was beyond the learned methods of abuse trainers had been taught for generations.

As new elephants entered the park, they would be adopted by one of the self-created herds. Each family brought in new members across generational lines and each family protected their own family unit, none more so than the young ones. During meal time people and elephants alike would clamber under the feeding structure. The humans stood in lofted walkways surrounding the feeding area, waiting for the unloading of melons and bananas which were then offered up to the waiting herds by park visitors, volunteers or staff. Bath time was possibly the greatest delight. When it was time for the daily baths humans and elephants made their way down to the river's edge, at its most shallow point, and guests assisted in the washing of their larger companions with elephant-sized brushes and soapy suds. The sound of splashing inevitably roared in the background as the babies of the herds did flips, flops and full somersaults as the river carried them past.

The evenings were full, as well, with delicious homemade vegetarian Thai food, and conversations about the day. Each day had a feeling of timelessness. The place felt timeless. I met a number of people from the United States while there, all who had been to the park more than once and called it their refuge from the world. One particular guest, a tattoo artist from Chicago recommended a tattoo artist back in Chiang Mai which I would find on my return trip and get a tattoo of an elephant family on my lower left calf. An addiction therapist from Los Angeles also came annually as his reprieve from his work in substance treatment. Each person was seeking their own bit of heaven in the valley. Always finding it, and always returning back to it over the years.

My first night of three in the park there was a terrible storm. There were semi-wild dogs who had made the park their surrogate home—adopted into the land and the park for all intents and purposes. By day, the packs would weave their way through the herds like pedestrians navigating traffic in Lower Manhattan, without any real concern about being trampled. The elephants, in their nearly infinite patience, tolerated their canine companions and the paw-full traffic jams. By night the dogs would find shelter under huts or in the grasses surrounding the park.

Rule number one, which I learned on arrival, was to not feed the dogs and do not let them into your hut. I tend to try to play by the rules in someone else's valley, and I generally heed warnings about wild dogs. I woke up in the middle of the first night in the park to the sound of my hut door slamming open. A huge gust of rain and wind had blown it out. As it opened, I saw two things. First, there was a large stream of lightning and rumbling thunder clapping simultaneously, lighting my darkened room for a moment. With the light came the view of a very large and furry figure making its way through the door and towards my bed. I was initially terrified at the sight of something slinking across the room tall enough to reach the bed. Then I was instantly relieved as my eyes adjusted and I saw it was a dog and not a more brutal carnivore. Quickly, however, I remembered the rule.

"O.K.," I cajoled with little conviction, "You have to go now. You are not allowed to be in here."

I tried to edge the dog towards the door like a matador corralling a bull.

The door was still flapping, and the rain poured into the small space. The dog backed away from me and the door as if to say, "Are you kidding?! I am *not* going out in that."

I tried to press my new bunkmate towards the door but as he moved away, the beginning of a snarl on his lips as he prickled with discontent, I remembered the words "semi-wild" next to the word "dog" in the early warning.

I replied to his non-verbal cues with a thunderstorm compromise.

"You know what, let's just call this an exception."

I closed the door, to forestall any further visitors, and figured we had a solid enough pact going between us. He wouldn't eat my face and I wouldn't make him go out in the rain. All of that settled I cautiously fell back asleep.

I woke up in the early morning to the drumming of paws on the aluminum roof of my hut. Walking outside I looked up and saw my nighttime companion, now like my personal canine rooster, walking tall and assuredly like no other dog I had ever seen in my life, on the top of my roof. Shaking my head at the absurdity, of the night and my morning alarm clock, I turned towards the railing of my stilted bungalow towards my view of the valley floor. Before that moment I wondered what breathtaking felt like. Mist coated the ground around me, creeping from the river's edge about 500-feet away and swirling like a vine through the air, reaching through the slats of my raised floor, seeking my toes. In the thickness of the smoky dew filtering the air around me I could make out a silhouette emerging. Slowly swaying and rocking, she appeared like a sunrise peaking from behind clouds. It was Mae Perm, I knew instantly, because the day before while her herd was bathing in the river it was explained that due to repeated abuse she had been maimed while working in the logging industry. For most elephants the inability to use one of their legs would have meant death—unable to walk they would just fade away into nothing or be killed by their owners. Mae Perm had taught herself how to move, how to stand, and how to live by creating her own rhythm of swaying and rocking, like a sacred dance of perseverance.

There she stood, in the morning mist, rocking along the river's edge, like a vision or a dream, in her own meditative trance. No one else was out, besides her mahout, and it felt like her story, in that moment, was offered up just for me. A private vision, a sacred prayer, a wordless translation of what I had been struggling to manifest in myself—the ability to walk, even if wounded by life, by trauma, by violence, and the ability to persevere and find the beauty in the dance of moving alone. She reminded me that there is beauty in the woundedness, there is sacredness in the scarring, and there is nothing to fear from the rhythm of walking alone. She reminded me that we can find the balance to move and to be and to exist even when everything says we should more likely fade away than survive. Our life is our own story and our greatest adventure. Our ability to move, even when everything against us says we should just fade away, is a miracle we contribute to making come true.

I followed the park for years after that visit, and still do. There is something about that place that always beckons my soul to return. Someday, I will. I learned recently that Mae Perm died in her sleep in April of 2016. I am forever grateful for the grace of her presence, lent to me in the silence and secrecy of an early morning mist. It changed my journey, immeasurably. It taught me to walk my own way and find my own rhythm.

FLASH-FORWARD: LEARNING TO WALK

Nearly a year since the Camino, over six months since the divorce, and I was driving north again during a sweltering southern July—just me, a Hyundai, and two dogs. This time I was traveling from Asheville, North Carolina to my second plot point on the way to Chicago where I would be moving at the end of the summer. I was headed back to New Jersey and to my parents' house. After almost a year in flux I was fairly certain I was giving my dogs their own attachment trauma. I was headed back again to the home of Crocheted Mary, where I had my first good skinned knee private shower crying session and launched my compulsion to private pain.

I was going back this time because my ACL tear from the year previous was now impeding my ability to walk without falling down. Apparently, this is a possible side effect of blowing through the meaty pieces that hold one's knee together. I was told a total replacement of my ACL was what was necessary to stop the near constant cases of me falling down and going boom all year round. The surgery and recovery process were supposed to be about a month which meant the much-needed support of loved ones. I was very grateful that I had parents willing to aid their convalescing daughter as she—quite literally—learned to walk again. This felt a little on the nose.

I mean really, God? Starting life over. Learning to walk. It was a bit obvious.

The metaphor pounced to life in the shape of a cadaverous ligament inserted into my knee. I wasn't about to question divine metaphor, however, and since I was falling down all the time and that just wasn't going to work, I rolled with it.

I arrived in New Jersey and promptly went back in time about fifteen years as I was stationed in my old bedroom. I began setting up as best I could for this surgery. I was forewarned by doctors and previous patients that the recovery would be intense. I had exactly one month before I needed to be able to drive the two days from New Jersey to Chicago with my two dogs. This meant, no matter what my body did or didn't want to do I had to be ready to drive a very long distance, walk and dog walk within four weeks or less.

Easy-peasy.

Then, you see, what happened was … I fell down, again. It happened right after I got to New Jersey and just a few days before I was supposed to have my surgery. This time on my side, the full weight of my body landing on my arm and doing something that seemed within a very short time to be at least a very bad thing. I went to the doctor. Like it was my hobby. They told me I had broken my right elbow. So, now I had a broken elbow and I was about to be on crutches within days, learning how to walk again with the full weight of my movement on my arms. This was getting particularly precarious and exactly the kind of plot twist my body likes to offer when there are deadlines and words like "impossible" being thrown around.

Ok.

So, I had one month to learn to walk again, to drive across the country with my dogs, and I would need to do it while leaning on a broken arm part and a recently replaced ACL to get the job done.

Divine comedy? I think, yes.

Me, my torn ACL, and my broken elbow limped our way into surgery. I emerged a few hours later with a new knee. There is something both renewing and terrifying about the obligation to learn and caretake for a new piece of yourself. One of the early forewarnings I received when selecting my choice of ligament, between a cadaver over live tissue, was that the surgery was less invasive, therefore a slightly shorter recovery time but also a likelihood of less mobility with the cadaver ACL. Meaning, as my doctor explained, my knee might never fully straighten again. As a yoga teacher and practitioner, I decided that this wouldn't do and set my own goal of full extension even with my new-old cadaver ligament.

The day of surgery I was in excruciating pain, but the thing about a ligament, unlike a broken bone, is stasis doesn't heal it, movement does. Also, I had a doctor who believed in immediate physical therapy and, so, by the day after surgery I was in the physical therapist's office, beginning my regimen of movement and extension which would prepare my new ligament to walk again.

On the first day my therapist told me, "It is literally as if this ligament hasn't been used ever before, so you will need to teach it to walk like it is the first time. We begin with making sure you can get the full range of motion. This is critical or you will never walk without a limp when it heals."

My life became consumed with the process of learning to walk. Each day I was re-teaching my body what it needed to know from my ligament and teaching my ligament what it needed to know to function. Besides the two hours of physical therapy four times a week, I had to do home exercises twice daily for about one hour each time. In addition, I had to ice my knee with a mechanical ice machine that pumped cold into my knee to make sure the swelling didn't overwhelm my mobility. Beyond that I had a massive machine which extended and bent my knee for an hour at a time, three times a day. I called this my "knee meditation" machine because of the exceedingly slow and rhythmic way it moved my knee up and down at increasing levels of extension and flexion each day. This meant every day was entirely focused on various methods of healing this one small part of my body that I realized was so critical for the functioning of the whole. All this was done with my internal time clock ticking down to the month mark when I had to be capable of driving to Chicago—just me, a Hyundai and two dogs.

I have never been much of an athlete. See ACL tear while at post office for the beginning clues as to why, but with my body of illness and injury and a lifetime of procedures and surgeries, you could say the sport I excelled in is recovery. I recover like a champ. I can push through pain, exceed set recovery goals, and hit the marks ahead of time. In some ways it was an amazing relief, after six months of wading through some of the most emotionally painful and exhausting periods of my life, that I could focus on something so literal.

At the same time there was also something profoundly powerful, in this most emotionally broken and uncertain place, to rebuild my life from the knee up. This life after divorce and the loss of everything I had known began with learn-ing to walk again. Camino was gifting me in the most appropriate way my life could a sneak attack pilgrim journey. Through physical brokenness and recovery, I would find my way to my new path of life. Each day, through each therapy session, as I learned to walk again, my body restored something in my soul. Like that day with Mae Perm in the valley where she reminded me to find my own rhythm to walk my own way, my surgical recovery reminded me I had the stamina, capacity, and perseverance built inside me, to stabilize myself, and learn to walk again.

It was excruciating. It was exhausting. It was everything starting over should be.

Being able to embody my restoration and find my equilibrium was so difficult if someone had laid out all the steps in specific before I started, I would have wanted to give up. First, I began with simple movement, then with crutches aiding my steps, and finally into walking without assistance. Sometimes it is just about getting off the floor, first. Stopping the flow of tears shed at the feet of a Crocheted Mary long enough to remember you *can* stand. Then, little by little, you relearn how to walk. It will require new parts and it will hurt a ton, but you will be stronger than before. You will be more than restored. You will be rebuilt. You will be reborn.

One month later, as I made it out of the driveway of my parents' house with my Hyundai, two dogs and all my crap, as well as a hefty brace down the length of my painful but mobile left leg, the driving away felt different than the two times before. The first time, in Boynton Beach, I was leaving an entire life with no knowledge where I was going and feeling a loss of everything I had left behind. The second time, when I left Asheville, I felt the weight of the surgery and recovery journey ahead, as well as the uncertainty that I would be able to learn to walk again. The third time, I was moving forward on legs I had worked hard to move forward.

It wasn't quite liberation yet, but it was the start of something new. And it still hurt. There would be recovery time left ahead. I was told that the recovery time for an ACL to fully repair was about a year. I was, also, told the same amount of recovery time was usually required to really heal from a divorce. Regardless, for the first time in a very long time, I was standing on something that felt like a solid foundation. I *could* walk again.

And, by week four of my recovery, I had begun to extend my left leg completely again, despite medical predictions otherwise. Like I said—I am a champion of recovery.

THE PRACTICE: Walking Through Pain

The practice for this chapter is to consider what your pain is right now that you feel most deeply—that you can't see through. What would it look like to walk through? What would it look like to learn a new way to walk—to move you through that pain?

Which tools and what strength do you need to build up to make walking through it seem more possible? Where is the small step you can begin with?

Do you need to build courage? Do you need to build self-worth? Do you need to build a sense of self? Do you need to find purpose?

What are some small ways you can build the muscles for that task? Taking a dance class to feel more confident? Taking a long bath to feel more self-nurturing? Imagine building on that practice—making it a part of your life, like a practice, like physical therapy for your soul.

Consider ways to bring to life your own inner strength and consider embodied— tactile, experiential, body-oriented—ways you can engage with that strength.

Sometimes using our own physical self to build our emotional and spiritual strength can be deeply empowering.

CHAPTER 7

Soul Mother

ON CAMINO: A SAINT, A FESTIVAL AND A WALLED CITY

I DID NOT expect to limp my way into Ávila, on the 500-year anniversary of the feast of St Teresa, but also, of course I would. How else could I come into the place of my naming, of my patron saint and soul mother of pain, and out of pain, other than with a hobble?

Well, first it was a hop, then a hobble.

I had a sleeping hull for the overnight train from Santiago to Ávila which meant I had to find a way to balance my weight and my pack, shimmy into the narrowest room, up the narrowest ladder, to the hobbit hole of a top bunk which was my assigned sleep space. This would have been difficult enough for my clunky and traditionally clumsy self but with a massively swollen knee, unknowingly torn ACL, and a hiker's backpack stuffed to the brim I am surprised I didn't just give up and sleep in the crevice between bunks at the base of the sleeping cell. Getting out, however was even more of a painful endeavor. It was a hop, and a thump, and a whopping amount of shooting pain, followed by a hobble, first off the train, and then by taxi to my little inn, Las Leyendas Hotel, set right at the exterior of the majestic and mythic walled city that is Ávila. *Las Leyendas* means legends, and even through the intense pain, as I paused between the courtyard and the door to my room, looking up at the walls as the sun slowly yawned into the early morning, I thought of the implication of being at the feet of legends.

It was the city of Teresa of Ávila and John of the Cross, who radicalized their lineage and secretly rebelling against their existing orders. It was the city of late-night passage by mule to escape the gaze of Spanish inquisitors and those that would do them harm. It was the origin of the founding of a life and an order that would put limb and reputation on the line at increasing levels of danger, eventually seeing John locked up in a tower, tortured by his Carmelite brothers, and escaping in the dark hours of dawn with a small dog at his side. It was where Teresa confronted God after a rainy night's fall off a mule. When they said, in reply to her fall, "This is how I treat my friends," she replied, "And this is why you have so few."

It is the city where Teresa was caught, late one night, devouring a partridge in her monastery kitchen, and when asked by her Carmelite sisters why she was so unrestrained she said, "When I pray, I pray. When I eat partridge, I eat partridge."

I always took this particular fable as free license to pray and enjoy life with equal intensity. These were my legends and the stories I had grown up on and into in my mystical developmental years.

It also felt like coming home. While I could only make an educated estimate that the city of my birth was Bogotá, I had always known that the city of my naming was Ávila. This city had been a part of my story longer than anything else I knew for certain. Arriving at 6:00 a.m. in most pathetic physical condition, I knew I needed a nap, but nothing longer. I had only one full day in Ávila (due to transit delays at both ends of my Camino), it was the 500th anniversary, and Teresa and I were going to enjoy this party as only a couple of Teresas could. This particular party would be a hobbled, exhausted, and emotionally-wrought fiesta for two.

Before my nap I decided a shower was in order. I was terrified to take off the compression bandage from my knee knowing from the level of pain what the situation might look like under the hood and being of the mind that what you can't see won't hurt you, or at least not have immediate dire consequences. I peeled away the bandage in the dim light of the marbled bathroom and with each layer I pulled back it exposed a new brimming heap of swollen flesh, desperately trying to escape its corseted cage. By the time I had removed the whole thing I could see that the entire center of my leg was double that of its counterpart.

"It's fine," I thought, which was just the kind of platitude I would make my mantra when I knew everything was not fine.

"It will be totally fine."

I finished a quick shower. The speed was mostly because injury plus balance plus slippery surfaces have never been my friend and then promptly fell into a bed that was gloriously unlike a hobbit hole, falling into a delicious sleep for a couple of pain-loosed hours. When I woke up it was about nine o'clock in the morning and the sun was gushing through the windows from the courtyard. My left knee was as corpulent as a cherub, but I was glad to see it wasn't any dire hues of blues, which would have been the one cue I felt I couldn't ignore. Since it was only disgustingly swollen and not swollen and discolored, I took that as a sign that no medical attention was needed.

I shoved—ahem, I mean, kindly and gently slid—my poor knee back into its corset casing and tried the best I could to not let the level of pain I was feeling overwhelm my excitement for what was ahead, or at least not overwhelm my basic level of brain functioning. It was rounding the last few months of the year-long celebration of Teresa's 500th anniversary but the energy around her festivities hadn't been dampened. There were maps everywhere marking the various Teresian exhibits scattered throughout churches and buildings across the city and flags commemorating the landmark on the streetlamps and flag-poles of every block. I was getting into the energy and loving the enthusiasm. I was containing my own enthusiasm in the cadence of a brisk and steady limp. Each step served as a reminder that internal energy can't always be matched by external output. In my case, for me and my body, that was almost always the case. This time, it was just really, really evident. I would have to pace myself, which I categorically hated doing, if I was going to get through this day. Body of a tortoise, heart a of a hare. That was the short summary of my eternal struggle and maybe a great title for a book on chronic illness.

I reached the first exhibit and just inside the entrance a movie was playing, with a few rows of seats set up in front of the screen. It was an artistic short about the life of Teresa and as I sat down, my knee immensely grateful for the reprieve, I felt like I had really arrived. I made it through Camino. I made it to Ávila. I was making it through my knee. I was really here. Not like in my life where I was often this solitary wild mystic nerd adventure inside my head. I was in a city alive with Teresa's life, in a season where the central focus for an entire populous and its visitors was her story.

Starving my whole life for a return to ancestry in some form or fashion this felt, at the very least, like a step back in one dimension of my own history. Yes, incomplete. Yes, absent the social-cultural analysis I would later do which would problematize my mystic heroine in the life she lived. It was, however, a beginning of knowing where I came from in a visceral way, that I had been seeking since I was a little girl running my finger over the black and white sketch of an unknown woman on a postcard in my baby book. If nothing else was true and certain about my roots, I could trace who I was back to an orphanage full of baby cribs, an order of nuns, and a woman who came from this city. For an international adoptee, that was more than many others had available.

After watching two rounds of the short film I negotiated the prospect of standing up with my left leg and with some momentum and a grunt and made my way forward. The movement was slow, painful, but also quite gleefully. I had never seen so many Teresa artifacts or really knew such things existed. Around each corner of this church turned exhibit hall the walls were covered with centuries old oil paintings of Teresa: Teresa with John of the Cross, Teresa and John with Jesus. It was like an old-fashioned version of an Instagram album.

All the permutations of a life remembered and artistically rendered lined every wall and coated every corner. I spent the day walking through the exhibits, church by church, building by building, seeing the intimacies of one person's existence through so many different eyes, over so many centuries. My final stop of the exhibits inside the city walls was the Iglesia-Convento de Santa Teresa de Jesús which is a functional convent for Discalced Carmelites (the order of Carmelites Teresa founded) beside the church which was built on the ruins of her childhood home. Interior to the church is what is called the Chapilla Natal, a space off the main sanctuary just before a small prayer chapel built in memory of Teresa's childhood. It is set in a place believed to be close to where her room would have been, in the direction of the wall and the hills she would have looked out on daily as a girl. Outside the church and along a side street is the entrance to the Museo de Santa Teresa where the permanent collection of artifacts of Teresa's life and works are held. This whole series of experiences, housed within one small city block, was by far the most sacred of my entire day in the city.

Inside the walls of the church everything slowed down. I was able to just sit, in meditation, in each of the spaces in this timeless way in which I wasn't worried anymore about how much day was left and what was still to be done but allowed myself just to be without urgency to be anywhere else. I spent time in silence in the main church sanctuary, then made my way to the room set as Teresa's childhood room which was a replica of how the space might have looked in her time. For a long while I stared out the window, at the views of her sky and her sight of the wall. I looked down to the little patch of garden where a statue of a childhood version of her had been sculpted and imagined her playing her games in that garden. This is where she would pretend to be a nun and create a little monastery with other children in her garden.

Then I moved into the chapel past her room, transfixed from my first hop through the door. Flickers of gold gleamed off the walls her life was painted on, in scenes, in panels, moving upward towards the high ceilings. At the central altar there was a large statue of her with outstretched hands, and pews to every side. I sat down and sunk in. I let my leg ache but released my attachment to the level of pain and went inward, particularly grateful in that moment for years of education on non-attachment to suffering as taught by my Buddhist teacher. As the pain grew in severity over the course of the day, I needed the paradoxical grounding in my teachings on letting go to allow myself to rest inside the pain without centering it. I closed my eyes and released everything that wasn't serving me in the presence of that moment.

Like the walls of the cavern at Santiago the air sung with the vibrations of prayer and reverence. As I sat longer in silence and in the mystical space of breath and pain, I also felt the air hum, as if whispering, without words, in the intonation of Teresa. There was a merging of time and place, pain before and pain after, pain mine and pain hers, memories mine and memories hers. I couldn't see or feel the distance between us in that space of silence and in the darkness behind my eyes. Wordless interconnection wove through every particle and cell of my being in a way that no panicked conversation or prayerful request ever had, so fully. I was in her and through her, and she was in and through me. There was no space between.

Time was gone.

Space was gone.

The illusions between us were gone.

A sudden zap through my leg awoke me from the trance of prayer, not being sure if I had been there for minutes or hours. I got up but it was a slow and groggy awakening. Not like a groggy after a nap, but after the movement and shift across a great distance. I was recalibrating again to the here and now. I spent a few more moments in awe of the art and the love of Teresa etched into the space, before I steadied my legs and hobbled back out onto the streets, heading towards the wall at the edge of town. I had one more place I wanted to go.

As I limped my way outside the wall about fifteen minutes later, I looked into the distance seeing the sun already moving slowly downward in the sky. My eyes searched, yearning, in the direction of Teresa's monastery. This was the space in which she had spent most of her life, home base for her radical Carmelite reforming expeditions, home to the rooms she prayed and wrote and voraciously ate partridge in, and where she experienced most of her most beautiful and excruciatingly divine revelations. From my map I was unclear exactly how to get there or for certain how far I was from the point I stood, but I was fairly certain it would be between a twenty minute to an hour walk one way. There were no taxis in sight, and I had no knowledge of how to access one on the especially quiet street where I stood. I took a deep breath, pushing through the pain that stood in defiant opposition of such foolish notions as walking, and began to make my way down the steady decline that made up the remainder of the street ahead of me. Half way down the first hill, feeling like my knee refused to budge on principle, I called on my soul mother once again for guidance.

"Teresa, I need some help. My body is saying stop, but my heart is calling me to your convent. I'm actually too tired and delirious from pain to figure this one out on my own. I just need your cosmic brain download. What should I do?"

I paused, took another deep breath, and she quickly emerged with her reply as clear as if she was standing next to me.

"You have come far enough, my daughter. It is time to rest. You will be back, again, soon enough."

I felt a sudden rush of gratitude at the sacred permission to rest. I knew my knee couldn't take much more. Truthfully, it was probably far past what it could take, and I had no idea how I was still standing. I also knew cosmic time is not human time and soon enough indicated no exact course of return. Soon by divine standards could be a stand-in for "before you die." At that point, however, I didn't care. I just needed the permission to stop. Also, it was the first time Teresa and I ever spoke where she called me daughter. Something about that word, in that city, at that moment. I felt I had reached the necessary end of this particular story line. I had come here seeking my soul mother and in turn she had claimed me as her daughter.

I turned left, what I was pretty sure was the direction around the wall to where my hotel was and grunted my way back to my room. After convincing my knee to leave the bed again, a few hours later, insistent that dinner was a necessary course of action, I made my way up the stairway at the back of the hotel leading to the interior and then exterior dining area. The view was spectacular in its simplicity. The outside seating settled along the edge of the wall right outside the entrance to the walled part of the city, illuminated by yellow-tinted spotlights directed towards the peaks. I sat there for an hour or so, drinking a glass of red Spanish wine, and watching all the life of the city moving past. Even though my knee was telling me it was time to go back to the States, I also knew I had found a new-ancient home in Ávila.

FLASHBACK: THE CLAIRVOYANT CIRCLE

I was 32-years-old, married and living in Boynton Beach, Florida. It had been four years since my endometriosis diagnosis and about a year since we had started trying to get pregnant. While my biological clock was swinging ambivalently into incertitude on the idea of baby-making my husband's was certainly right on time. Due to my Stage 3 categorization of my endometriosis I had always known that getting pregnant would be a difficult if not impossible endeavor. Over the previous decade or so my endo had blasted its way through my reproductive organs like a tanker on a warpath. I had already had two of my four laparoscopic surgeries since we had started trying to conceive, as it was suggested by the doctors it was best to clear out the baggage of scar tissue that blocked and eroded the pathways necessary for eggs and sperm to run their proper course towards a uterus. I had seen one reproductive endocrinologist for the purpose he was titled for to help with reproduction. I had been seeing reproductive endocrinologists for years but, previously, that was because the only doctors that specialized in my condition were the ones in the more lucrative business of fertility.

During my initial visit with this particular doctor, after all requisite tests had been done to check the status of my parts, he told me, "You have a perfect uterus, it's just with all the damage to your fallopian tubes and ovaries, nothing can get there."

Part one of my response is, this was the first and only time my uterus had ever received a compliment. So, thank you to him for that. Part two of my response is, of course. My body is a war zone. I didn't need a medical opinion to know that was true.

After over a year of actively trying to have a baby, preceded by years we didn't count of just not-not-trying, was getting desperate. This felt especially strange due to my pregnancy and child-having ambivalence. It was like the stubbornness of a body that wouldn't do this thing, the historical indoctrination that my body was in fact built for and "supposed to" do that thing, and my own stubbornness which said no one would tell me I couldn't do a thing had all boiled to a scalding stew of inadequacy and impotence which I just couldn't bear. This was the peak of my war with my body. In my mind, it was bad enough that I had to be in pain every day for most of my life, now someone was telling me there was additional punishment for my troubles. I refused. I just refused to be beaten, and so it became a battle I would win, regardless of whether I wanted to put my flag on top of that particular hill or not. The point was, I wouldn't be beaten. In many ways I was like United States foreign policy since forever, except the battle ground was my own body.

Besides, I was a woman with an amazing uterus. So, that had to count for something.

I bought sticks for everything. There is a market for making sticks for every aspect of fertility. Someone is getting mega-rich off this market. Peeing on sticks became my newest compulsion. Sticks for basal body temperature which would tell me when I was fertile. Sticks for pregnancy, to see if I had gotten the temperature stick and penis stick game rightly coordinated. See it is not just enough to pee on the sticks, between all the urination you have to also leave ample time in the month for the other stick—the that in the best of times used to offer a semblance of fun and intimacy and had become one of mechanics and science. My body, my days, my experience of my body in every day, became a giant petri dish meant to prove the experiment that I was capable of being a woman in the way that everyone and everything said I was supposed to be.

Forget about the fact that I had spent much of my adult life believing in the fact that women were much more than their organs, that they had no obligation to birthing or parenting, and that every principle of my ideology said that this was a totally dysfunctional means of existence. It didn't matter. I had crumbled under a weight of expectation—internal and external—which had been hidden in the shadows of my subconscious. The whispers told me I was unworthy, not enough, and a failure if I couldn't get my body to do this one thing that it had been biologically crafted to do. Hell, even my birthmother, who had forgone the parenting part had been biologically able to do the manufacturing the fetus part. This felt like the greatest insult to injury. I couldn't even do that. My only piece of medical history I had known to me was that I had no maternal history of infertility. I was failing, at a biological level, my own family history.

I had a complicated relationship with the ideas of biology and giving birth for most of my lifetime. Spending years in mirrors trying to find the traces of my own biology—lost to me by the absence of biological relatives to claim me—led their way to an emotional adolescence. One where I felt totally lost. With no frame of reference for who I should be, or where I came from, I became obsessed with the ideas of my past and my future lineage. Beginning a short-lived experimentation with cutting at sixteen I remember a very cold midnight on my sixteenth birthday, sitting outside of my parents' house, on the edge of the backyard, holding my belly and weeping. I had spent the hour previous in my attic bedroom in the attached bathroom, carving out the letters of my birth mother's maiden name "Mateus" on my belly, just above my navel. I don't think I was intentionally inscribing my biological past on the only place I could birth a biological future, but it is not lost on me now. I sat there weeping, on this birthday that was supposed to be a landmark of "becoming" by some developmental standard, less sure than ever about who I was.

That following year, I became very prematurely obsessed with the idea of parenthood. I would imagine getting pregnant and when I had a few scares in my senior year of high school related to some really sub-par sex education mixed with an undercurrent of subconscious sabotage, I remember feeling a bizarre mix of elation at wondering if I might be pregnant. I also remember the disappointment when I found out I wasn't. Talk about really sub-par sex education, it wasn't until years later that I would realize that it would have been nearly impossible for me to have been pregnant, especially as someone who had been taking birth control for medical reasons since I was fourteen. The joke of infertility nearly two decades later left me realizing that I could have done anything with anyone, anywhere, and the likelihood I would have ever had a baby would have been slim. At sixteen, however, all I really wanted was a connection to who I was and where I came from, and my subconscious mind, knowing there were no roots before me, became unnaturally obsessed with building roots through a next generation.

Twenty years after my adolescence, I found myself sitting on the porch steps of a different home, weeping late night tears of womb inadequacy and feeling the rush of that compulsion and urgency of a biological tether I thought I had shaken off through years of hard work and emotional self-study. This made me not only weep for the baby that wouldn't come, and what that would mean for the lack of a biological lineage forward, but it made me ache for a birthmother

I had never known. It made me remember, all over again, like a grief resurfaced, the increasing chance I would never know a biological relative. I would never see a face that looked back at me like a mirror. I would be alone in this one way that didn't matter so much to everyone who had it available to them and mattered like nothing else did to those of us without it. Biologically, no one came before me, and no one came after me. I resented everyone, in that moment, who took their own biological tethers for granted.

It made me feel the urgency backward and forward with such intensity it felt like whiplash to my soul. I had searched for my birthmother years before and still felt the sting from the dead ends in that ancestral searching process. I called my orphanage FANA on my eighteenth birthday, the day I was able to legally get access to their records. The nun in charge at the time gave me what little information they had on record which included my mother's cedula number (like a social security number), her full name (which I already had), and the age she gave birth (which I already knew to be twenty-three). The nun on the other end of the phone told me they had no records of existing siblings and no information on my birthfather. No one had a birthfather in those days of record-keeping. In such a very Catholic country as Colombia, you see, everyone was an immaculate conception.

She also warned me with words I am sure she believed to be wisdom, "You don't need to be looking for these things. You have a family. You have a life. Why do you need to look back?"

If only she had known. So much of my life was looking back, searching for something and someone I might never find. I spent two years and two private detectives, following that phone call searching in Colombia for my birthmother. Turns out the cedula number she had given was a fake. It led the detectives to a man who had died years before on the west coast of the country. There was one lead that seemed to be validated. Sometime after Alicia, my birthmother, had me she did live near the west coast, in the Huila Departamento (district) to the direct east of Cali, where she worked for a local mayor's office. After that the trail of her life that followed was untraceable.

So, I gave up. I began to let go of the idea that I would find any roots history or discover my ancestry with any certainty. Then, at twenty-three, the year my birthmother gave birth and gave me up, I stumbled upon my first book of Teresa of Ávila, *The Interior Castle*. This would begin a love affair with the woman I would come to know as my soul mother, who would fill the places of sadness, emptiness, and uncertainty with love and familiarity. She would fill my broken heart with home.

It really wasn't until I couldn't go biologically forward in the face of my own infertility that I began to go back, again. It brought a sadness at either end of my lifeline. I felt the acutely finite nature of myself. I was just this life. There would be nothing before. There would be nothing after. I was a genealogical stump with no roots and no branches. As this reality set in and the sensation of living life as a dead stump began to consume my identity. I had worked so hard to answer the questions of who I was and whose was I, even without a history to teach me any of those answers, but once again my sense of self was being eroded away by this feeling of nothingness. This sense of being so finite propelled the procreation machine forward and fed this compulsion to conceive in a way that was, in the least, decidedly unhealthy.

I had started going to this place called *The Open Circle* over the year that fertility became my life's focus. It was a cozy little women's holistic center inside a refurbished bungalow house in the center of Delray Beach, Florida. It was a place attended mostly by moms, pregnant women, and the women who wished to be pregnant soon. This was already not really my crowd, but I was desperate. I had tried every medical technique and every herbal concoction that humankind and the internet could manifest. I was looking for the impossible answer to this consuming question, "Why can't I get pregnant?"

The owner said I should attend this circle group she hosted every month. There would be a clairvoyant coming, she told me, and it would be a good place to try to get the answers I needed. Normally, "no," with an additional side of "no, thank you," would have been my answer. I was a huge believer in the mystical, but I found that it was the rare public person, who charged admission for their offerings, especially to desperate and vulnerable audiences, who were the real thing. Not only that, but collective displays of mysticism were not really my game. However, I was desperate. Due to this manic level of desperation, I paid my $35.00 online and signed up to go.

I entered the room the following Thursday night to the creak of old wood under my feet. There was a hefty smell of incense burning in the background, and the dim lighting of candles cascaded over the wood floors and the small gathering circle of women who were taking places on the encircled cushions laid out on the floor. I took a seat nearest to the door, somehow feeling comforted by my easy access to escape, and waited silently, and yeah, kind of judgmentally, eyeing the women that entered the circle one at a time. They were mostly what I expected—white, middle to upper class women in their thirties and forties. They reminded me of the kind of women that were holistic in the way that Lululemon is yogic, all about it as long as it was high fashion, high cost, and low output.

They were harmless enough, but also seemed exactly the kind of crowd that would come for this kind of thing because of its exotic allure. It would be something to chat about over an over-priced glass of wine later, perhaps had while on a boat. I knew women like this because I had watched them being raised beside me, in my wealthy suburban hometown, by mothers of the same lineage and practice. I knew them because those same women from the Northeast all came to Southeast Florida for the winter. My whole life was haunted by this type and my inherent outsider role within their space. I was always the brown girl, with frizzy hair, whose diction could "pass" but whose social conscience and genetic complexion never quite could. This fact I was resentful of and hurt by in childhood, but so grateful for in adulthood. Now back in a room filled with folks I had spent the better part of my life working to not be trapped in space with I took a deep breath. It felt just like home, in the worst of ways, and also exactly where I should be when I reached my infertility desperation bottom.

A woman walked in alongside the center's owner, swathed in so much flowy fabric I was certain something was going to catch on a candle. She was wearing the exact right costume to play the part of the clairvoyant. "Here we go," I thought, "The show is about to begin."

I was brimming with skepticism and possibly a good dose of resentment. I was angry about being this desperate and for bringing myself into a room like this with women I spent my life trying to avoid. I was especially resentful for paying $35.00 for the humiliation. The flowy fabric clad clairvoyant sat down and began with her introduction and then a few instructions.

"Bring into your mind someone, alive or dead, who you would like to communicate with. As we go around, I will ask you who that person is and then we will see what shows up. I don't embody that person, I just connect with the energy and messages they have to offer," she said in that sort of wispy, soft voice that seemed just right for the caricature she seemed to embody.

One person at a time, women went around in the circle, naming someone they wanted to connect with, mostly dead parents or close relatives. I listened, each one seeming fairly rote and predictable responses were offered for each. About two-thirds of the way around the circle she got to me.

"Who would you like to communicate with?" she asked.

"My mother," I replied.

I did this both because it was true and also, the skeptic in me set it as a trap, wondering which one she would pick, not knowing I was adopted.

"Which one?" she replied, startling me almost off my yoga pillow.

"Ah, um, my birth mother," I stammered out, still totally unprepared for her clarification and specificity of her question.

She had set me off my game so much I hadn't even known for sure that's the mother I wanted to talk to until I said it. Mostly I had picked mother as my person because I was having a mother-type problem, and because I thought the clairvoyant would give me some bullshit answer.

"Let's see," she said, pausing and doing what seemed like listening.

"Here she is. I can't be sure if she is alive or dead, that is not how the messages come, but it feels like the energy is alive," then she paused again.

"She says, 'I am sorry we could not be together. We are both like fire and together we would have burned each other out.'"

This hit me hard in many ways. One, because the words about Teresa of Ávila always reflected on her as a saint on fire, and two, because I always had this inclination, due to my own intensity, that my birthmother was like me. I had this feeling in my gut throughout my life that if she had raised me it would have been a disaster, for both of us, for that reason. I was raised by calm and even-tempered parents who were capable of balancing out my own flames.

The clairvoyant continued, "She also says, 'I am a manifestor, and so are you. We were made to manifest in the world.'"

The second statement felt so true it seared right through me. In that moment I had no idea whether this store-front clairvoyant was legit or a sham, but I knew, from the specific language and content of the message, that the message was true. Specifically, because the second statement answered my question in a way I hadn't yet had the capacity to ask.

"Was I meant to give birth?" This question had become my obsession.

But manifesting is birthing without the need for biology. A manifestor gives birth and life in a different way. I have spent years rolling over the words of that message, not sure how they shot through this unlikely moment, with this unlikely conduit, in this broken place in myself, but their truth continues to unravel at each new step of life. It was a repair and healing of a lifetime of pain. Those few words offered me both forgiveness and a release for both my birthmother and me. It freed both of us, in my conception, and offered us the permission to be the mothers we *could be*, not the mothers we *should be*. It gave me the ability to see that we could both burn with the flames of our own, and that those flames were actually the connection of our whole and true selves, beyond biology and across time. It was the very beginning of me being able to grieve and let go of this idea of motherhood that I "should" have or this parent-age that I "should" be connected to in a particular way. It released me from my prison as a genealogical stump and allowed me to envision how I burned, and how what I manifested could live beyond my finite life.

FLASH-FORWARD: LINEAGE & FUTURE-BEARING

Two-thirds of the way through my first-year post-divorce and exactly a year after Camino I was back in the hills of North Carolina coordinating a spirituality festival that was primarily born out of, and cultivated for, white Progressive Evangelical Christians. Quite the niche! I had ended up in that universe much due to my work around healing and trauma and this would be my first year after my book came out specifically on spiritual trauma, *Sacred Wounds*. The communities of liberal-oriented spirituality, across traditions, are often filled with those who have experienced deep harm, previously, in more conservative religious contexts. This community was no different.

Spiritual trauma was something experienced deeply and widely in the community that went to this festival. For me coming to events like these was like a view into another culture. Because I was raised Catholic, in a liberal town and raised by liberal parents, I hadn't experienced the level of emotional and spiritual violation so many others had in conservative religious environments which were rife with homophobia, sexism, and bullying of difference en masse. By the time I was sixteen all of my friends would have identified as "queer" although no one had yet reclaimed that term, so we floated between the language of gay and bisexual. When I wrote *Sacred Wounds* explained clearly that my primary trauma was sexual trauma and my spiritual violence was more one of frustration and ideological disillusionment, not one of personal persecution or abuse. So, being in places so full of the experience of spiritual violence and violence by religious leadership felt like walking into someone else's world. It was a place I could be of use, but not one that necessarily felt like my own spiritual home.

The year following my divorce I would be returning for the first time in four years without my husband and without the community that I had brought with me over the previous three years. What would be equally surreal is that I was staying in the same house I had rented with my husband, our community, and his soon to be wife the previous year. At the time she had just been a community member at the spiritual community I co-founded with my ex in Delray Beach. Walking back onto that mountain and into that house felt like revisiting old ghosts, ones that I hadn't yet fully exorcised, particularly because they were not really dead. I was treading an old path but with an entirely new life, one I didn't know the shape of yet. Right after the festival I was set to fly back to New Jersey where I would be having my ACL surgery the day after I touched down, so my mind was also moving forward, into a different unknown.

One thing that pulled me back into that festival space was the excitement of a program I was helping to coordinate, bringing some of my own spiritual home onto that mountaintop in the form of a mystical gathering preceding the actual festival. Honestly, I could have stayed for just that and been quite fulfilled. Thanks to the coordination efforts of a friend and colleague, Adam Bucko, the gathering would include a number of mystics, including my beloved Teresa's beloveds—Tessa Bielecki and Mirabai Starr. They were two women who, unbeknownst to them, had saved my life and my spiritual journey many times over with their works and words on Teresa as well as the mystic journey as a whole. I felt deeply connected to their words and deeply grateful to be able to connect in person. It was a gathering of mystical foundation-keepers, who were also the keepers of my own foundational spirituality, in a foundation-less place in my life.

Both from time in community and conversation with them, over sacred space at meals, and other encounters along the festival road, I was reminded not just of the mystical texts that had sustained me in my darkest places but of the living embodiment of those texts. I was reminded of what was possible, not just in some mystical theoretical past that I could romanticize without full seeing. I was refreshed in the fact that we existed in the midst of a mystical present—one that we chose how to live into. The wisdom of two women who lived and loved, who felt the ecstatic pull of Teresa as I did, and who had made it through their own brokenness to find their way along their own sacred road also reminded me that embodying our own mystical path could look a thousand different ways, and was never, ever easy.

The time on that mountain reminded me it was possible to not just survive but thrive beyond the worst of things, even sleeping every night inside the house filled with the ghosts of my past. Being in that place at that time with the collection of mystics that surrounded me reinvigorated my own spiritual fervor and began to set a course for where I would go next on my own spiritual journey. It was also the last time I would go to that festival. I realized that, as Tessa had said: grief rewrites your address book. It doesn't mean that what came before didn't have a purpose but what was coming next needed space to grow—and that often means making the space for new things to breathe life.

In that space of fertile mystic soil, I had my first conversations with Jade T. Perry about what would later become Mystic Soul Project, the nonprofit we would co-found with Ra Mendoza to center people of color (POC) at the intersections of mysticism, activism and healing. I had become tired of being on the periphery, facilitating other people's spiritual communities and practice while my own had become anemic. I had also spent years in dominantly Christian-centric spaces, which were also often white-centric, where so much of my mystic experience, ancestral seeking, indigenous reclamation, and POC-specific traumatic experience had to shrink or disappear to fit into the box of "contemplation" that was labeled in black ink with a big do-not-touch sticker over the top. The year of struggle from pilgrimage to divorce through to surgery had taught me not just to let go of what wasn't serving my life but also that it was alright to begin to demand what I needed in the world. As I was also beginning to realize, even from those early conversations with Jade and a few other POC mystics, it wasn't just an otherness and alienation I felt as an adoptee or as a recovering genealogical stump. It was an experience of and expression of the forced smallness of so many people of color.

On the fertile ground of that particular mountaintop the genesis of an idea began to form, one born of the exhaustion of a life that not only had made me feel not-enough but which had proffered me a life of not-enoughness in return. I wanted more. I wanted to be my whole self—without shame or blame, without compromise. I was tired of fitting into other people's boxes and serving the needs of a dominant and domineering spiritual whole that didn't even begin to reflect critical parts of myself. I wanted to be able to be all the parts as an Indo-Latinx queer disabled woman and for it to be more than enough. In that moment I began a commitment to build a world in which that could be true, not just for me but for all people of color and queer/trans people of color.

THE PRACTICE: The Grief Rewrites

The practice for this chapter is to consider how grief, loss, pain and suffering has re-written parts of your life. What have you had to let go of to make room for something new? Who have you had to let go of to make space for something healthier? What parts of yourself that were no longer serving you or were baggage on your back and not assets to keep you walking have you had to discard to move into something new?

Whenever we let go, even of what isn't serving us, grief comes with that process. Grief rewrites our narrative but then we must grieve, also what we lost along the way. We need to take time to grieve and to let go—it is a process. If we don't take time to fully process our loss, speak it and experience it, then we will either repeat the pain in some other way or it will stay stuck and lodged inside, a barrier to whatever new might be on our horizon.

Take a bowl and fill it with water. Write on sheets of paper what you need to grieve, what you have lost, what you have had to let go of. Each thing on a different sheet of paper. Drop the elements one at a time in the water and let the paper dissolve. Leave it in there as long as you need to, and take time to process in writing, drawing, or dialogue with others, what you are letting go of and what it means to you.

You can do this practice individually or communally—communal processing of grief and letting go can be powerful and healing as a practice. We live in an individual world, but we need our beloveds with us on the journey—alone and together, at the same time. When you are ready you can take your paper out and throw it away - or if you need an extra oomph of release you can let the paper dry overnight (what is left of it) and burn the remains the next day.

CHAPTER 8

Setting Your Soul on Fire

ON CAMINO: LEAVING ÁVILA

LEAVING ÁVILA WAS very difficult. I mean yeah, of course, metaphorically, emotionally, and spiritually, but *literally* it was really difficult to leave. My knee had begun to veto the act of being a knee and it took about ten minutes of emotional cajoling and staring at my stuffed backpack, to finally convince my arms to comply with lifting the pack. They were steadily working in concert with knee-on-strike to forestall its inevitable suffering. When I finally swung the bag on my back my brain began to agree with them and almost convinced all of us, we were just going to live at the edge of the wall for an indefinite amount of time into the future. Regardless of the mounting strike, I had a flight out of Madrid that evening and a train to catch to get me there beckoning me forward and so I set out with my mantra in hand: it'll be fine, it'll be fine, everything is fine.

It was a little under two hours by train to Madrid and from there I had to hop, hop, hop to another train would take me to the airport. I arrived in Madrid without incident, unless you count my increasingly debilitating injury as more than incidental. The problem was that when I got to the metro-hub I couldn't find my train to the airport. Each step was becoming unbearable and yet I wasted so many of them having to move back and forth from track to track, up and down escalators, and through turnstiles that eventually locked me out of re-entry. After almost an hour and with a leg that was about ready to burst from fiery pain, I stopped in the central hub of the station, dropped my bag, and began taking deep breaths. I had the distinct feeling an entire nervous breakdown was brimming right at the edge of my quivering lip and watering eyes. I had walked my way across a portion of Spain. I had hobbled my way across all of Ávila. Yet I was about to be undone by the Madrid train station. That alone made me want to scream in the center of the station until someone did, in fact, cart me away to a hospital. I stood there breathing for what probably seemed like a creepy amount of time and then said from myself to myself, "You can do this. You are a capable human being. You will not lose your mind in Atocha train station."

Just as I said those words on the inside of my skull the outside of my eyes looked up to see the electronic message board light up with the words "Aeropuerto" and a track number. It was the track right across from the one I had exited an hour previous. With that combination of relief and rage you feel when the simplest solution appears right when you are at the end of your sanity, I stared down at my bag and wondered if I really needed to bring luggage back home. Then I remembered the Teresa icon and Camino rosary tucked in my bag along with a number of gems hidden in the piles of unspeakably icky clothes and, sighing, I picked up the bag. I just reminded myself, to myself, that it was almost the last time I would have to do it.

I arrived at the airport just in time to check my baggage and say goodbye to that particular feat of spiritual flagellation realizing I had been carrying around my own little torture device in the shape of a too-large blue backpack for far too many days. I mean, again, I know that pain can be a powerful spiritual conduit, but I was not all about the cat-o-nine tails type of body punishment unless of course was between two consenting adults. Even then, I'd personally rather not. In that moment, I was happy to never carry my personal penitent backpack, again. Also, I have never been much for the whole self-abuse for the love of the divine dynamic. A parent who wants me to abuse myself to win their love is not one I would stick around long to build relationship with. Letting go of the backpack for me was its own spiritual release. Yet I did have this feeling that I had, in some way, earned my way to the end of my pilgrimage. Not because some vengeful God needed me to, but because I needed to prove to myself the value of this journey. It mattered and I hadn't given up on completing my journey. I had found my way to the feet of my saint, my soul mother, my lineage-keeper.

I was especially grateful when I was given a row with extra leg room at the front of the plane. That felt like a divine reprieve after a long and painful journey. Pilgrimage has that ability to create its own timeless bubble where the course of a week's travel can feel so vast and transformational it is hard to capture it in the number of days or the literal hours that had passed. I settled into my roomy aisle seat and stretched out my aching leg, glad for the forced rest of a nine-hour flight from Madrid to the States. I was able to sink into rest for the first half of the trip but woke up with the sensation of stretched and numbed flesh throbbing around my kneecap. This is when I realized I was in trouble. All the pain and exhaustion had made me forget a very critical fact of long trans-Atlantic flights and injury swelling. It was hella dangerous, medically speaking, and sometimes even deadly. I had forgotten that pesky science of combining swelling and elevation. You know, the one that makes doctor's disallow their patients to fly after surgery or injury. Except of course I hadn't had a doctor to remind me of that fact. I had an ace bandage care of La Farmacia, which didn't come with such warnings and reminders. Right about this time I began panicking remembering those stories I had heard about swelling and aneurysms, or was it heart attacks? Ahh!

I lifted up my pants and saw that the swelling from my knee had expanded exponentially. I was swollen down my left leg into my ankles and feet. Everything swollen to double its size making what once had looked like a limb resembling an unsightly Frankenstein monster appendage. This is also around the time I realized my feet were beginning to fall asleep from the pressure of swelling toes inside now too-small boots. I began to loosen my laces and try to wedge my left foot out as quickly as I could, worrying if I waited much longer, I wouldn't be able to move it out at all. As I bent down to do this, however, another equally horrifying realization crept in. My right leg was also feeling that stretching sensation. Not wanting to know, but knowing I needed to check, I pulled up the leg of my pant on my right leg and saw that the swelling had expanded not only to my entire left leg but my right as well. My whole right leg was swollen to nearly double its size and my toes were equally suffocating in my right shoe. I rushed to get them both off my feet. As I tried to stretch out my legs and bend them for circulation, I realized neither leg would bend. They were both too swollen to move.

I was beginning to feel like someone had put a pox on both my limbs in Shakespearean style. I couldn't move my legs. Due to the numbness and circulation impairment from the swelling I could barely feel most of either leg. This led to a realization around basic human functioning and my current physical location in a plane seat. Let's say I didn't have an aneurism or a heart attack (whichever it was I was in danger of) I was not going to be able to walk myself off the plane. I took a deep breath, although I was no longer able to muster any one of my soothing mantras and hit the call button for the flight attendant.

When she arrived, I said, "So, here's the thing, I got this injury during my travels and now both of my legs are so swollen they are mostly numb and twice their usual size. I am fairly certain I can't walk as I can't really feel either of my legs or move them right now. First, could I bother you for some ice? Second, I believe I will need some kind of assistance when we arrive at the airport because I am fairly certain I won't be able to get off this plane."

I was pretty impressed with her nonplussed flight attendant facial expression as she replied, "Of course ma'am. We will take care of that. I am so sorry for your distress."

I couldn't read her airline poker face well enough to know if her cool demeanor meant I should worry less about blood clots, or whether she was just really good at her job. I figured either way there wasn't much I could do about it. I would ice my knees and hope I made it to the States where, apparently, hobbling home was out of the question. We finally arrived in Charlotte, South Carolina, where I had a stopover before my final destination in West Palm Beach. I was so grateful to not have combusted on the plane I wasn't nearly as humiliated as I thought I would be by needing to be assisted off the plane and wheeled through security.

When it came time for bag collection, however, I sat in my chair and looked over at my other West Palm-bound wheelchair companions. They were all in their eighties. Of course, they were, we were heading to Florida. As I looked over, I realized they were all eyeing me with discerning eyes that said, "What do *you* need a wheelchair for?" Me, a young, and externally healthy-looking whippersnapper. I could see they thought I was faking.

I smiled politely and thought, to myself, "You all have no idea what kind of mess this body is on the inside!"

Also, if I picked up my pants in that moment, which would have been weird to do, they would have seen how very not good I was on the outside. It felt like my body was manifesting the symptoms of the effects of the pilgrimage. My external suffering and transformation embodied in my hopping, swelling mess of a body was expressing something at work in me on a much deeper level. I was awake with the pain and beginning to wake up to the state of my life, the unhappiness of it, and the necessary changes rumbling in its future. One more plane ride and another wheelchair liaison got me to my husband, who got me to my house, where I would recoup from the external swelling for another couple of weeks. The internal rumblings, however, were just beginning.

It was only four months away, at that moment, from my impending divorce and the detonation of my life as I knew it, but in that moment, I already knew something was shifting. Pilgrimage does that. It stirs life up and gets you moving in directions you need to go, but often aren't quite yet ready to venture towards. The road to real life transformation doesn't always start with a bang. Sometimes it begins slowly, with a wheelchair and an airport escort.

FLASHBACK: WAR TRAUMA & INVISIBLE WOUNDS

Catastrophe is often the catalyst for great change. The full circle of our life's journey is, ultimately, about the return. We come back into our lives, changed and transformed, in a way that shakes loose the life we are living while creating an entirely new path forward. My journey through my own experiences of sexual trauma, post-traumatic stress disorder (PTSD), and recovery was one of the largest transformational processes of my life. Definitively the most transformational process to that point in my life spanning from late teens to mid-twenties.

In full, the cycle of transformation was a long and protracted one for me. Much of that was due to years stuck in the pain-avoidant and static limbo of my PTSD and stuck inside a cage my mind had created to protect me from a pain it thought it couldn't handle. When I began to wriggle loose, after having dropped out of college, moved halfway across the country to Colorado, and engaging in a very unhealthy romantic relationship to try to escape my own internal prison, the potency of my aliveness was overwhelming. It felt like I was awakening from years of slumber, and in many ways my brain and body were doing just that. I had been on hold when the pain of my trauma had felt like too much and when my systems were back on line they were so intense it was almost a sensory overload.

I wanted to do everything I had missed out on, but more than that I wanted the return from my suffering to have meaning, not just for me but for others. I figured all that time in pain couldn't just be wasted time, it had to serve something beyond my own self. This propelled me into a tunneled mission to help those who were as hurt as I had been by trauma and assist others in finding a way out of the prison of PTSD with a better map than I had.

This also meant returning from Colorado, where I had been living the past three years, back to New Jersey, moving back in (temporarily) with my parents, and going back to an undergraduate degree program to finish the four-year program I had abandoned when the intensity of my own trauma began to swallow up anything that that had previously had meaning. In a hurry to make up for lost time, I crammed as much coursework in as I could, completing the bulk of my remaining bachelor's degree in two years of nonstop classes, transitioning in January of 2006 from my completed B.A. to an accelerated Master's program in clinical social work at New York University. The program was 16-months in length, and I would have to complete it in four back-to-back semesters.

On orientation day, we were sat in a room and everyone was given an envelope with a slip of paper inside. Each person's paper articulated their internship assignment for the first two semesters. I had asked for something working with sexual trauma or domestic violence, feeling that was where I wanted to end up professionally. I opened my envelope, first eager, and then nauseous. Inside there was not the name of a sex crisis center or a domestic violence shelter but instead it said: Department of Veterans Affairs, Vet Center - working with combat veterans with PTSD. To that point I had not known anyone that served in the military besides my cousin who served in the National Guard during peace time and I could think of no kind of trauma I was less equipped to help, and no population I was less capable to serve than war veterans. I was a pacifist, after all. What would I possibly be able to do to help these warriors heal from something I was diametrically opposed to in the first place?

"This is gonna be a disaster," I thought.

Two semesters of this internship turned into a job offer after graduate school and that job became my work for the next eight years of my professional life. I learned more from working with veterans about the human cost of war. I was exposed to the deeper roots of the need for peacemaking, beyond my surface pacifism, *because* of the cost to the people I served. The existential casualties of war were as deep as any physical wound, in some cases more insidious because of their invisibility. I was also given the ability to see the equitable nature of all human suffering and trauma.

My pain was not theirs, but we had each fought the wars of trauma and PTSD. Seeing inside of their pain made me understand my own even better. Seeing inside of their pain offered me the gift of compassion and the honor of serving warriors, not because of some blind loyalty to a nation, but because of the bravery and the values the people I served held. I always said I would never find clients like vets again in my professional career. Veterans held the values of trust and loyalty so sincerely that any one of them would have jumped in front of a bullet so it wouldn't hit me. Because we had a mutuality of trust earned and pain seen. I learned from them a compassionate peacemaking which I never would have been given without the guidance of their lived experiences, their humanity, their pain and their trust in me. I walked alongside them as they battled their final war, the internal struggle of invisible wounds and the ghosts of battles long gone but preserved in time and engraved on their souls.

The costs of war are never as great as for those who have to face it and live with its consequences. Every battle I have had in my life has made me reflect on that work and those people whose lives which were interwoven with mine for the better part of a decade. There is nothing more powerful, spiritual and existential as looking into the heart of the suffering of war and walking with people through that pain.

It was not the place I thought I would find the purpose and meaning out of my suffering, but like many journeys that start with a gulp of fear and trepidation, it was exactly where I belonged. It was the only place I could have learned so well to be a guide for others through the heart of suffering and out the other side.

FLASH-FORWARD: STANDING ROCK & MYSTIC SOULFULNESS

It had been three months since I had moved to Chicago and I was getting used to a radically new lifestyle that included things like a bed of my own, an address, and a closet. I was slowly getting settled with a rhythm of life that included a return to full-time school in a Master of Theology program at Chicago Theological Seminary and was in the process of transferring my social work practice license to the state of Illinois to begin a local practice. While my life was beginning to settle some, the nation around me seemed to be going through its own transformation and upheaval.

We were at the beginning of what felt like a pilgrimage of national proportions without a clear endpoint to the disruption in sight. The work on the frontlines of justice was becoming simultaneously as empowered as it was chaotic and painful, reminding me of the work on my frontlines of combat trauma. My national work, as the world had shifted and my life as well, had bent itself more and more towards these intersections of worlds. All of a sudden, my own life's journey through pain and my work through the pain of war had a new frontier (social movements) that appeared more aching each day for the understanding of where these two worlds of trauma and transformation met. Additionally, since the upending of sanity and political realism with the national elections having just emitted a particularly harrowing result, the machine of justice and activism was kicked up into a necessary frenzy, unsure of what the fates of all peoples in the margins would be.

For myself, both in my studies, my life, and the surrounding sociopolitical sphere, I was centering on my own beginnings. I was beginning a journey of reconnection with my origin story, and what it meant in the moment to be a brown woman in 'Merica. I was also considering what it meant to be a brown woman who was still finding her way to her whole-self-authenticity. After having lived the years of my marriage much like those of my childhood, a brown woman in a dominantly white world, often suppressing the parts of myself I most sought to know, just to be palatable enough for my surroundings I was over it. I was tired of glossing over or tamping down the fullness of my response to the subtle and gross racism that pervaded so many of the white spaces I spent my life swimming in, as if it was alright to be "racially impolite" as long as you were in the majority in any given room.

Breaking out of the casing of my world as I knew it also meant I could break free of shackles I didn't even realize I was wearing. The ones I had on in some form or fashion my whole life from my white suburban upbringing to my white contemplative community of learning to the whiteness inherent in my marriage and life in Florida. None of those things were anyone's "fault" per se, I had just learned so well how to navigate a white world I realized I hadn't allowed myself to fully inhabit the skin I was in or explore how I wanted to own that, without the gaze of whiteness informing the performance or presentation. In that process of suppressing my whole self I had also never sought out the peoples of my origin.

I left behind a large part of who I was when I gave up the search for my single person lineage in my birthmother. Something about the quakes of my life and the quakes of the world around me made my brown skin more visible in the world and more essential in engaging the fullness of myself—mind, heart and spirit. The narrative landscape of my whole life was pulsing alongside this world aching with the pain from the margins, the struggle to be seen and valued, and this call for healing into the midst of the struggle for justice. I still couldn't see the whole vision of where I was being beckoned, but I felt clear I was on the precipice of knowing and was listening for where I needed to go to get there. The pilgrim's path shows up in our life, as our life, and we have to figure out where the Camino arrows are in our living, breathing world. They are not nearly as easy to find in the distraction and detritus of the everyday, but when one does show up in a place of transition you know that you need to say "yes."

One of the places of justice meeting healing giving me hope with increasing frequency and increasing media headlines was the work happening at Standing Rock Reservation. Slowly at first, a community of protection had formed at Standing Rock, standing in the face of the builders of the Dakota Access Pipeline. It had begun with only a handful of people and with little news coverage in April of 2016. By November of the same year, the numbers of people showing up to stand in the face of this pipeline, threatened to build a leak-likely pipe under the water supply of an extremely impoverished community of Lakota people, had grown exponentially and continued to grow by the day. The urgency of their plight had also increased due to the impending presidency of the 45th in the White House which threatened to overturn any efforts to bring a legal halt to the pipeline process.

This movement which had started with a small collective of local Lakota-led organizers and organizations had grown to the thousands and had seen visitors and new community members joining the struggle from tribes around the world and communities traveling by car and plane from all over the United States. As I began to follow more closely, I also wanted to see what the mental health care needs were and the existing support on the ground. I was amazed to see that this community, built out of a movement, had become an equipped mental and medical support network with an ethic not just for the care of its community members but also of the indigenous-first model of how that care and community was offered up. I was profoundly moved to see that all medical and mental health care providers coming in to provide essentially crisis care were mandated to learn the indigenous care methodologies, herbs, and local remedies as the first line of defense. Regardless of what western, colonized practices of medicine a provider came in with, they were to have reverence and deference to the wisdom of the peoples of the land. It was even more poignant and important given that this was the same wisdom that was stripped away generations ago, by the same system that now propelled forward poison for profit into the natural resources of the same peoples.

I also realized that with the "holiday" of Thanksgiving looming ahead, there would be a surge of additional people in the camps, and with the physical resources depleted, there might also be a taxing on the resources of care. I had a week off of school and the capacity to travel, so I began to think how and if it might serve for me to offer up what I had (my trauma training) in service of the critical work being done at Standing Rock. The temporary community was offering an example not just of movement community at its most powerful but also indigenous reclamation at its most potent. This was something I deeply sought to understand, as someone who had never been given permission to seek, let alone a roadmap to find, my own reclamation of identity. I took a long time to discern whether I was going to be of help or not before I made my choice. I wanted intentionality and my own ethic as to how I would enter into any healing space, or whether the answer to the question was that I was not needed at all. After a long series of internal conversations and periods of pause, waiting to see if there was an arrow calling me forward, I realized that what I could offer could be a useful support. I also committed to give more than I took, and with my intentions solidified, and my yellow arrow pointing north, I began making plans for the journey.

I decided to go for a full week and worked within my communities in Chicago and around the country to raise funds to bring supplies to support the community. I also brought everything I needed for my own care so as to not tax the existing ecosystem of life and decided to collaborate with a team capable of supporting the transit of goods to the camp and who were called in the same way to give into service what they could to the work at Standing Rock.

It was amazing how quickly the funds were raised to support the journey. My own community, from my local Chicago folks to those across the country, gave to the endeavor. It also reminded me that, often, when you get called into a necessary "yes" there is this amazing synchronicity of the world opening up to that yes and nurturing its becoming. In total, there were eleven of us and four cars which headed out from Chicago in the direction of North Dakota.

I left a day before the larger group with a team of two to get set up, acclimated, and also to help as soon as possible as I was going with a specific role of mental health support, whereas many of the others were going to plug in to support as needed when on site. Much like every Camino, it was very much a world of alone-together.

My team of three people—a fellow student Kate, a violinist Yelley and myself—arrived late at night and the winding and convoluted roadways were almost impossible to discern in nearly pitch-black darkness. We accidentally found ourselves on a wrong street taking us directly to the one place no one wanted to go. Right in front of us, with no turn subtle turn-off available, was the paid militia barricade set up by the Pipeline to keep water protectors (the movement's term for their community of action) out of the area. As we pulled up, close and tight to a barricaded entrance to the water protector camp, there was no way not to see the extent of firearms being held up by no less than half a dozen large men. They were loaded up with weaponry equal to the task of quelling a mass insurrection, riot or combat frontline and they were wearing intentionally deceptive military-style gear, making their paid enforcer status seem regulation military.

As we pulled up, we devised a plan to play the part of ditzy and harmless girls lost on the way to the casino. Since there was a casino about five miles back in the opposite direction, it was late, and they were armed it seemed the best course of action for our own self-protection and safety. It was laughably clear, as we smiled sweetly and wove our tale, that we were not headed to any casino that didn't include a resupply center and a camp-out option as our car was loaded with every manner of camping equipment along with a crap-load of supplies for the camp. They nodded and smiled in response, also doing it through their own set of laughable lies about why the road was blocked due to bridge weakness and construction. We parted ways, with them giving us instruction towards the "casino" which also was the direction we needed to head for the camp. We all smiled and waved through the farce of our circumstances, each of us knowing we could be face-to-face in a very different way in the near future.

We finally arrived at camp at 2:30 a.m. and to front gates that looked like a fairly well-fortified security check point replete with flood lights on the street and guards at the gate. I would learn later that the guards were mostly a mix of retired combat veterans and members of the American Indian Movement (AIM). This combination actually brought me a sincere sense of safety. Both those groups knew what danger looked like and how to mediate it. I had never before tried to setup a tent in frigid North Dakota November on a darkened path of snow and it turned out to be exactly as difficult as one might imagine it to be. The ground was partially frozen, and the stakes refused to go in to the stubbornly resistant cracked earth. As we struggled, I realized we had become the premonition realized of ditzy girls in the snow. Two men walked up just as I was about to give up and suggest we do sleeping bags in the hatchback.

"Hey, do you all need some help?" one of the men asked and as soon as we said yes, they set to work setting the entire tent up for us in amazingly quick time.

I have never been so grateful to fall asleep in the freezing cold or quite as shocked to wake up in the pre-dawn hours to the vision of icicles dancing over my head. Turns out, if it is cold enough not only do you have to sleep like a mummy, with only a breath hole open from your sleeping bag, but you also wake up to everything covered in a frost and ice. On the inside of the tent.

Everything from my breath hole to the entire interior of the tent walls was covered in a layer of frost and tiny icicles. When I woke, I had the bodily sense that it would likely be warmer outside my tent in even more clothing with my body moving than it would be inside. That, however, was not what woke me up. What woke me was the sound of a car driving by with a man on the bullhorn, calling as he would each morning before dawn, "Wake up relatives! It's time to pray! This is what you're here for!"

He drove around the entire length and breadth of the camp, in the flatbed of a truck, shouting this call to prayer which convened daily at the sacred fire in the heart of the camp. The fire was lit on the first day of camp, in sacred ceremony, and would stay lit for the duration of the movement community's existence. It was also the spot of many community gatherings, the daily announcements, and all morning and evening prayer and ceremony. It was Lakota-centered, Lakota-led, and others would only enter by express invitation from the Lakota leadership.

They were unabashedly who they were, holding their community and the visiting community, with love and kindness but also authenticity. They were unwaveringly rooted in and through their people's way. Their ownership of their whole selves, without asking permission or waiting for it, was a profound representation of something I unconsciously hungered for and seeing it expressed was an inspiration for what was possible. I had spent my whole life being palatably brown, constantly bending myself to fit into the framework of whiteness. From my contemplative spirituality world, to my mental health professional world, and into far too much of my personal world I had been bending to acquiesce reflexively for so much of my life. I had become so bent I didn't even know how to stand tall, but I was learning, from the first day in camp, what it looked like.

That morning around the sacred fire I felt the warmth of bodies holding a circle of prayer in the dim light of dawn and the harsh cold of Dakota winter and I was given a glimpse of ceremony that wasn't tethered to a colonized conception in any form or function. It was inherently earth-bound, connected to ancestral and indigenous rituals, and wasn't even remotely referential to what it was opposing, rather intent on standing in the truth of what it stood for, even as the specter of a militarized frontline was almost visible along the horizon opposite the fire.

The land itself, its harshness and brutality, the remnants of a continent once unowned, compartmentalized by a colonizing mentality insistent on owning everything of beauty and leaving the degraded parts for those who came before. The people of this land persisted in spite of that, not afraid of the cold but embracing their natural world in all its truth. They held this truth in the cold morning dawn as they held the circle, tightly, with honor and always with prayer. I would learn from that first morning that everything in camp was about community, prayer and healing not despite the movement and activism that buzzed at its core, but because of it. Everything was interconnected. Spirituality, activism and healing were a symbiotic web, and without the fullness of one, all the other parts suffered.

I had known this intersectional symbiosis was true at an intuitive level that I could now call also an ancestral level, but inside of the silos of western-colonization and its progeny I had been struggling so hard to find the rhythm of this symbiosis. I knew healing couldn't be complete without spiritual grounding (or grounding with beingness) and without connection to the suffering of the world around it. I knew that grounding and spirit-centering was hollow and shallow without being founded in personal healing and collective response to the suffering of the world. I knew that action in the world and the response oppression and violence would ask too steep a price of a person's heart and soul without being grounded in healing and spiritual centering. I knew these things but being mirrored back my whole life only the siloed constructs I had been given, being silenced in my own intuition, I had shoved down my natural inclination towards wholeness for partial truth packaged in good branding.

Inside this community, the parts didn't even need to do the work to come together to make a whole, they had always been the whole in the first place. It was a remembrance and a reclaiming of what was always known, and a lifting up of the inherent wholeness of this indigenous way, and specifically this Lakota way of knowing.

Prayer went on inside a timeless wheel that first morning as we stood encircling the sacred fire. I didn't know how long we were praying. The prayer curators were unhurried. Time held a different value here. It wasn't a commodity to be conquered and sequestered to pieces for profit and productivity. It was fluid like the river we walked to at the end of our time of prayer and ceremony, to honor the gift of water and remember why this call to its protection was vital.

Our first day was spent learning the community, as was the credo of the camp. Every person entering had to go to orientation, not just to where we were, but why we were there and whose land and struggle we were entering into. The emphasis of Lakota-first and indigenous-first was beautifully crafted into even the lifting of voice and who was centered. The camp spent intentional time deconstructing the paradigm of power and privilege with an explicit camp ethos of prioritizing indigenous voices first, then women and queer folks, and white straight men if there was time left. The power of this one practice was amazing and in the practicing of it, it brought discomfort to those who had less space, perhaps for the first time in their life. It also lifted up the wholeness and value of those who had spent much of their life having to make themselves small (or being made small) by a world that devalued their voice. After orientation in the morning there was a direct action training, led by the indigenous organizing group Indigenous People's Power Project (IP3) which facilitated a very thorough half day training, equipping people to engage in direct action specific to the land, the struggle, and woven together with the Lakota ethos of the camp. After the training, I checked in with the mental health teepee and found out about the daily meeting for clinical care at 8:00 a.m. that I was invited to join for the next morning. This is where my work would begin.

Over the course of the next few days I would spend day to night doing a variety of tasks related to mental health care and wellness in the camp. I did everything from providing an introduction to mental health care and trauma response at the direct-action trainings, to providing on site care in the mental health tee-pees and yurts (in which the lack of heat and lighting were always the greatest barrier). I offered mental health first aid to the direct actions at the river's edge and acted as sex education specialist with condoms in backpack and reminding folks to be safe due to a bit of a surge in what folks were calling "NO DAPL babies" at camp.

The days were long, but the work taught me more than I could ever synthesize fully about indigeneity, authenticity, reclamation, community and dignity. It also reaffirmed my call, out of my own suffering and trauma, that my work in trauma—from combat to Standing Rock and later on to offer mental health triage in Charlottesville, VA—had continued value for the world I was living in. One in which the distinction between combat and activist frontlines in the political climate of a looming and then imposing Trump-era presidency would have very few distinctions. In many ways a new generation of my own personal inquiry into claiming my own indigeneity and an ethnographic study of my ancestry began over those freezing cold nights and ice-capped mornings in North Dakota, but so came a renewed sense that the work and knowledge of combat trauma would have increased purpose in a new kind of frontlines.

I also realized, by the example of the indigenous leaders at Standing Rock that I could unabashedly be exactly who I was in my own lineage—I could be the paradox of history and colonization brimming under my skin and in my story without shame. It would be a long work in progress, but I no longer reflexively felt not-brown-enough because my Spanish came from a high school classroom or defensively apologetic for wanting to hold and prioritize my brownness in white space. There was a model for ownership, even in oppression and under the gaze of a colonized circumstance, which I took away from the world of Stand-ing Rock camps that informed everything that came after—including a radical and honest analysis of what I needed in mind, body, spirit and community.

Ra, of the other team members from my Chicago caravan told me one evening near the end of the week, "I saw an indigenous man today, I don't know from what tribe, and when I first looked at him I thought 'That looks like my uncle.'

I never thought being here would connect me to where I come from, and my Mexican roots, but it has."

There is a Lakota phrase told to me by a colleague from Pine Ridge Reservation while we were working together on a project with the Indigenous Ministry of the Episcopal Church for education and healing related to the Doctrine of Discovery. The phrase is "Mitákuye Oyás'iŋ» which means, in English, «We are all related.»

When I heard the Ra's story, and felt the resonance and mirroring of my own belongingness in the indigenous-centered space of our Standing Rock camp, I realized there was something deep in my indigenous memory, in the history and lineage of my origin that pre-dated any particular biological parenthood, and spoke to a community of ancestors. That belongingness had been awakened in me at Standing Rock. It did not need permission to exist. It did not need permission to own itself fully. It had always been there, in me and through me, connected to my DNA, and activated in a sacred space of indigenous wholeness. That activated belongingness said these were, in some way, my relatives. It whispered into my heart the secret truth that had awakened something in me in the midst of sacred fire, circle rituals and the resonance of drums humming me to sleep each night from the center of camp.

We are all related.

In our pain, in our histories, in our oppression and our trauma. In our sacredness and our rituals. In our strength and our resilience. All of us, people of color, silenced and made small throughout a colonized history were connected. We deserved to be visible, valued and remembered for ourselves, for our peoples, for our past and our future.

A few months later I would officially found my nonprofit, The Mystic Soul Project, with my friends and colleagues Ra Mendoza and Jade Perry. Both people who had been present for some awaking of my wholeself-hood on my own journey. Both mirroring back to me our deep yearning to find and remember what was lost from our collective and individual histories. Both mirroring the resonance in the drum beat of our ancestors—we are all related.

Our mission and our calling were whispered to me in that "yes" to go to North

Dakota and awoken for me around the sacred fire—centering people of color at the intersection of spirituality, activism and healing. We *all* deserve to be our whole selves, and I knew that part of my new path out of pain and into transformation was to birthing space. I was a manifestor. My mother told me so. If nothing else I could stumble my way in the general direction forward and find others invested in the invitation to walk with me towards our unapologetic and radical wholeness.

Because "Mitákuye Oyás'iŋ.»

"We are all related."

THE PRACTICE: Passion's Progress

The practice for this chapter is about where your passion, your story, and your pain meet your calling. How has your life called you to be where you are now? Or how is it beckoning you somewhere new—to where you are going?

Consider your own story and its ebbs and flows. What are the landmark moments that changed you, and when did those moments change the course of your life? Sometimes we can change course in directions we want to go, and sometimes we have to make course corrections over time, as we can be set adrift in directions that are not our path. This doesn't mean, either, that there is one path only. Life is a bit of a "Choose Your Own Adventure"—you get to choose what happens next, and from that choice comes many different options, and that continues. Your choices today might not be the same as five years ago—but we can always course correct to find where life is calling us now.

Take a moment to write down the critical moments of life and where those transitions and transformation led you.

Then ask yourself if where you are is where you want to be. If it is, take some time to reflect on how this path is serving you and how you want to move into in your next step—write down some visions, dreams and hopes for what you can walk into next. If it is not where you want to be—go back and notice when you may have gone one way because it was easier, safer, or because it was what you needed to do in that moment to survive. Without any judgement of choices taken—sometimes we need to find what helps us survive before we can recalibrate our inner strength to find what helps us thrive. Then begin to consider, vision, dream and set hopes for where you would like to course-correct to—no dream is too big.

Wherever you are—on the path you want or looking for the path you seek—create a space (or spaces) in your home that is an homage to your story- sacred items, things of great memory, as well as pictures, images, words and reflections of what you want to vision forward—kind of a two and three-dimensional vision board, something you can see and touch, even smell if you want to add scented items to that space.

A sacred space just for your dreams—and where they meet what the world might need next.

A Pilgrim's Return

IT WAS THE summer of 2018 and the heat collected in the divots between the rise of hills along the Spanish countryside was bearing down with a dense but dry pressure on my skin. I could almost feel my skin sizzling as it was exposed to the sun sitting high in a nearly cloudless sky. I took a deep breath as I stepped off my train at the Ávila station. A memory floods in and I reflexively reach for my knee feeling the phantom pain three years prior when I hobbled onto the same train heading in the direction of Madrid.

Between those summers so much of life has changed. Married to divorced. Floridian to Chicagoan. And so much between it had changed. Even the way I was arriving in Ávila, Spain was distinctly different.

On my first arrival at the same train station, three years prior, I was cocooned in the privacy of my own thoughts. I was carrying my pilgrim's baggage, feeling the thumping of my own pulse radiating into my left knee without full knowing how much I was injured. I entered from a posture of solitude, carrying the magnitude of my arrival at the origin place of my namesake and a pressured expectation to find home and find the roots of myself.

Fast forwarding three years, I was arriving alongside the cacophony of a crowd. I returned to Ávila, much the way that Teresa had promised me on my last night in Spain, but I didn't return alone. In my absolutely characteristic over-ambition, I had decided to facilitate a fourteen-person pilgrimage to the city. It was the first year that the Mystic Soul Project was a fully functioning project and we had just completed our first conference that January. We had about five hundred applicants for attendance and nearly three hundred attendees for the first gathering which had blown me away. It was a collective mirroring of the need and hunger for a space of authenticity for POC, and a depiction of how exhausted so many folks were from spending so much of their lives in a world centered on whiteness. Out of that momentum and following the completion of the first draft of *Going Naked* I decided to plan a POC-only pilgrimage to Ávila.

I felt the inspiration to try this for a number of reasons. When I had first come to Ávila, I had been desperately seeking to find my own connection to ancestry in the city and its history. While my time with Teresa had been profound and a critical step on the journey that brought me to return, again, it was an incomplete story. Personally, the story of seeking Teresa in the Spanish mountains was one that sought a partially true history of who I was and whose I was. I was of Teresa, and I was of the Iberian Peninsula both spiritually and historically. I had discovered my birth mother's name of "Mateus" was actually Portuguese in origin and was also—fun fact—the name of a fairly famous Portuguese wine.

Even so, the Mateus I came from, Alicia from Colombia, wasn't only Spanish or Portuguese. She was brown and indigenous. She was the ancestral representation of genocide, colonization, and forced linguistic and religious assimilation. The story was more than the saint I had come to know as a friend and confidant in moments of pain and the woman that was Teresa came from the complicated origins of that history. I wanted to return to Ávila with a community willing and wanting to explore the complexity of our histories and our spiritual lineages. I wanted to return to a place of home and also complicate what it meant to even have the name Teresa—named after the Spanish roots of the Conquistadors who perpetrated harm on my own indigenous ancestors. I wanted to excavate the past in community.

Additionally, I wanted to offer the pilgrimage opportunity I had three years before to a cohort of folks who would never have made up the traditional demographic of European mystic pilgrimages. Those kinds of pilgrim experiences were popular in a specific subset of people who were almost inevitably white, cis-gender, heterosexual and fairly wealthy. Usually, the offerings came with very high price tags and that wasn't including airfare or accommodations.

No one I knew, including myself, could ever afford to attend those kinds of pilgrimages and I had never heard of one that, with equanimity and transparency, excavated the beauty and the complexity of Euro-centric mystical histories. I wanted to create a pilgrimage accessible to and created for people of color—one that was for folks of all ages, genders, sexualities, and socio-economic capacities. To make the last one a reality I raised money towards the funding of costs for the attendees and also made sure that I kept everything cost friendly in terms of our daily budget. Additionally, I didn't pay myself out for the facilitation which is often where the greatest cost to the attendee comes on the trip. In the end I was able to supplement the costs to the level of need for each attendee to make it feasible for anyone who wanted to come.

History Re-membered

In my own preparation for this trip back to Ávila I did a very different regimen of study. I researched the history of oppression and marginalization within the context of Teresa of Ávila's time (including about two generations in either direction of her actual time period). I studied the annexation and alienation of the Moors and what we would today call a campaign towards anti-Muslim and anti-blackness in her time and geographic location. I explored the correlation between that history and the literal walling of cities in Europe as well as reflected on the way this practice was parallel to our own "build a wall" propaganda and corollary hate speech.

I paralleled also the golden age of various societies that went from being robust and diverse empires to hate-mongering cultures of fear-based bias and legislation and found comparatives to this effect for the Golden Age of Spain that preceded Teresa's lifetime followed by the colonizing and bigoted era she was raised in. I built some comparative reflections about how this was reflective of a similar pattern in both Nazi-era Germany and Trump-era America.

I looked at the anti-Semitic swell of the generations preceding Teresa's lifetime and the very public shaming and forced conversion of both Teresa of Ávila and John of the Cross' fathers. Those that were converted were known as *conversos* and my psychological opinion is that much of the over-the-top "Catholicism above all" fervor of both mystics had roots in the lingering generational trauma imposed by the conversions and both their, and many other families, looking to erase the stain of being remembered as Jewish by becoming the most Catholic. Not just "make Spain great again" but "make Catholicism the best thing."

I uncovered that not only was Teresa's brother part of the early wave of Conquistadors and colonizing forces to the Americas but the funds that supported the founding of her first monastery came from that blood money. Not to mention the fact that the remainder of her funding throughout the course of her work to radicalize Carmelites came from the one-percent of Spain, the ones that were the greatest profiteers of the colonization of the New World during a time when Muslims had been eradicated from the land, Jewish people had been diminished by forced conversion or false imprisonments and executions. The world of the Teresian age was not unblemished and neither was her work in the world.

I had realized, between my last pilgrimage and this return to Ávila that everything and everyone is imperfect—myself, herself, anyone. We can't properly love something without seeing it clearly. I wanted to see this history of mystical lineage clearly. I wanted to love and forgive and remember and be able to hold the paradox of truth. The whole story of Teresa's lifetime *is* the lineage of my own story. The whole truth is both my story as ancestor to the oppressor and the oppressed.

As an adoptee the one way to learn who I am and whose I am based on the geography and genetics of my roots is to do a DNA test. A few years ago, I took the ancestry.com test and it showed that I was mostly indigenous from the Americas (interesting, genetically, the tribal differences are so discreet they don't register between tribes north and south). Secondly, I was from the Iberian Peninsula and thirdly, I was from Northern Africa. If you could draw a parallel of my history and ancestry it would have been the story of Spain. I didn't want to hold one-dimensional idealized versions of Teresa or of the roots of the mysticism I had come to love. I also wanted to offer a dimensional pilgrimage for a cohort of POC pilgrims.

Wrangling Cats & Lessons of Group Trips

We were a haphazard troupe of travelers, as we lumbered out of the train car and into the heat of the city. In the group of fifteen of us there were professors, activists, pastors, artists, students, and politicians. Folks had traveled from every region of the United States and came from roots that were African, Latinx, Asian, and Indigenous. About half of our group spoke Spanish and the people that did spoke it much better than I did. We aged from early twenties to fifties and across the spectrum of sexual and gender identities.

About five hours into the trip, which began in Madrid, I knew that no one person should facilitate a pilgrimage of fifteen people. However, one day into an inter-continental group trip was not the time to make those determinations. I realized I would quickly become the de facto tour guide, historian, EMT, Google map and logistics coordinator for anything, from the largest to the smallest need. I could tell that despite my personal overwhelm the trip, overall, found its way to become the pilgrimage I hoped it would be for everyone who had joined the trip.

I felt like the instant parent of triplets who is so tired by the end of the day that they don't realize until dusk that they put their pants on backwards. Regardless of my own delirium, I could see and hear from the people on the trip as they reflected over lunch or dinner, or conversations over a glass of wine in the evening, that they were having the kinds of experiences I had remembered having throughout my own Camino pilgrimage years before. They also deeply enjoyed the capacity to talk about the hard things—the real histories, the oppressions, and the ways they reflected the pains and experiences everyone was feeling in their current day lives in a Trump's 'Merica. There was a freedom of a POC-only space that allowed for a level of sharing in different rituals of prayer and ceremony and gave permission for folks to struggle with the hard things around their own identities and their lived struggles.

It was also fascinating to see the sacred sites, many which I had visited on my last trip, through their new eyes. I enjoyed seeing what they noticed and what had impact for them on their own pilgrimage journey. It was like having a window seat to someone else's spiritual process and I felt honored to be able to be in the passenger's seat as each of them found the meanings and messages meant only for them in the breadcrumbs of sacred object, memory and history along their path. I noticed, as well, that as I went to each place my perspective was dramatically changed. As someone who had just begun my own radical new monastic community through the Mystic Soul Project I was seeing through the eyes of a foundress.

While at the Teresa museum I didn't spend my time drooling over the first editions of her books, as I had the first time. I spent my time looking at the artifacts of the labor of building something—the floor plans, city documents, and the funding sources. I considered questions of resourcing and compromise, thinking about how you keep integrity and also keep the lights on. I thought about the choices Teresa made and what that meant. When we went to St. Joseph's Monastery, her long time residence and the building outside the walls I couldn't make it to the first trip, I thought about the exhaustion she must have felt as she collapsed on the nights she was able to sleep in her own bed under the weight of long days and the pressure of her project. I was seeing her life through the eyes of a fellow builder.

I was on a new stretch of road on my pilgrimage of life and I felt it distinctly during that trip—curated by me but not really experienced by me. I had become the tour guide to transformation.

We Get it to Give it Away

One night near the end of our time in Ávila I was lying in bed, stuck in an uncomfortable sleeplenessness. During our time in Ávila we were staying in the retreat house adjacent to the Iglesia y Convento de Santa Teresa. Each room housed a single person and all the rooms were set side-by-side going down long hallways, in the traditional dormitory-style for Catholic retreat centers. The rooms each housed a single twin bed, a small wooden desk and chair, a tiny arched window overlooking the rectangle of courtyard in the center of the building, and a small bathroom with a shower, sink and toilet.

I imagined my room like the equally small solitary residence Teresa spent most of her life in. As I lay, neither specifically seeking nor struggling against sleep, I remembered reading about Teresa's exhaustion, at a point, with the labor of the work. Always on the road, always fundraising, always building for others without time for her to have space and energy to give into her own sacred time. She was all output and no input. She also came to the conclusion that as long as she was called forward, she would continue until she felt called to stop. As a result, she never stopped.

She died because, at the age of sixty-seven, she had to go to the birthday party of the child of one of her donors (you know, like a celebrity appearance). Since they were a large donor, no wasn't an option. She traveled on mule in poor weather and by the time she arrived she was already sick. She never made it home and died in a stranger's bed, miles from home.

Something about this story frustrated me. I was tired. I had been persistently tired for years. I have continued to be persistently tired. For. Years.

Part of learning Teresa's life and historical context has also been about being able to healthfully separate the human and flawed woman who was a product of her time and her ideologies with the mystical patron I have known in my own life. Our ancestral guides are the perfection of their human selves—the characteristics that made them, them retain. This is also why I think my patroness Teresa shouts f-bombs in my head. I like to think a contemporary version of her would have done the same thing. She has Teresa character, but she has the wisdom of eternity the living Teresa in her own time could have never had.

In that way, I am not sure of the ethos of the Teresa of her time—dying for a funder and working without pause. To me this is emblematic of the same ethos I have seen in activist spaces and religious spaces where, somehow mixed up in a Western capitalized structure of productivity, we have conflated calling and a compulsion to work. The real-life Teresa gave me a model for breaking down what doesn't work and radicalizing what needs to be busted through. She gave a good model for following your own mystical path and listening to the depth of the divine in our lives. However, it was post-mortem and mystical patroness Teresa that taught me to, "Shut the fuck up, sit down and rest."

Pilgrimage take two also planted the seeds for that lesson as well. I lay in my twin bed, exhausted from my output, while also reassured by the impact of the work on other people's spiritual lives and journeys. I realized the real work was going to lay in the tension of finding the balance between my first journey to Ávila and then the return. Life is not entirely input, but it can't be all output either. No one can sustain a life of all labor and no sustenance. Sure as hell not in chronically ill body. No wonder all the mystics had medical issues.

I was given the gift of pilgrimage to give it away.

We are given any gift to give it away.

Which also means, in the giving and abdication there is loss. I did everything over the previous years of my life to get to the point where I could build a community for folks like me, seeking spiritually-infused POC, could seek and be in their own authenticity. I had to own my truth and my story, move through my own pain and suffering, face my demons and my mystic patrons, so that I could offer up what I learned in service of others. However, when we give it away, we lose something, too.

Yes, of course, we gain much, but I hadn't realized that the sense of loss would also be as palpable. Even so, I know that loss is just a cleansing. Like pilgrimage and the journey of life has taught me, we clear the way, and unstuff the backpack of what we have been carrying so we can make room for something new.

I pause.

I breathe.

I take a moment to reflect.

And I wait to see what will enter into the space made by what has been cleared away. In the meantime, I will just take the next step, and know that even if I can't yet see through the fog to the clearing, soon enough the next yellow arrow will show up to guide me forward.

ACKNOWLEDGEMENTS

WHILE THE INITIAL process of book writing might be a solitary practice, the making of a book to publication is a collective endeavor. I am very grateful to the many people and communities that have given into the creation of *Going Naked*. This book was profoundly personal and intimate for me in ways that I couldn't have imagined when I began writing it and I have lived into new chapters of the story as it was being written. In that many of the thanks for this book are deeply personal as well.

A big thanks to Marisol Lado and her daughter Ariana (Ari). Marisol for being a companion on the Camino journey, but beyond that, being a friend to me throughout so many turbulent times of both of our lives. We have gone through weddings and marriages, divorces and relocations, and maintained connection across miles and years. I am grateful to her walking on pilgrimage with me, way beyond the Camino road. I am also grateful to the hilarious and sincere contribution of Ariana in this pilgrim's story and the tiny backpack that could and would have, had it needed to.

Also, a thank you to Jose Antonio Lado and Dania Lado who gave me a safe place to land before and after Camino in the hillside above Santiago. To Jose and his willingness to courier us towards pilgrimage, even if he never quite understood why we were intent on doing that five days walk. To Dania who offered me a bed to land in, food to fill my belly and for the immense gift of a laundry for which my grimy pilgrim's body thank you and, likely, so does anyone who had to stand in my radius.

I am thankful to all the many mothers that have carried me throughout my journey, from skinned knees to more serious knee injuries. To Patricia Bennett I am so grateful for how she has walked with me as mother every step of pain in this life, to my grandmother and her lilies, etched on my back in tattoos, to my birthmother Alicia Mateus, and to the many Teresa personas that have shown up when I needed them the most.

I hold deep love and gratitude towards two mystic women, two friends of Teresa, and beautiful authors on the mystical journey. Through their own reflections on Teresa and writings out of their own life's journey they have been mystically maternal to me in written and living life. Thank you to Mirabai Starr and Tessa Bielecki who, first through their writings on Teresa, and later in their presence as elders, companions, and teachers in my own life have grounded my own mystic journey and been present with my travels with and through Teresa of Ávila, and the evolving journey of my own soul.

I am very grateful to those who have assisted in the making of the mechanics of this book. To my mom who is always an early reader and first editor of everything I write. To Ra Mendoza who served as my real time beta reader of each chapter of this book as it was initially crafted – their feedback was essential in considering the chapters and especially influential in considering the addition of my epilogue – as they felt the story wasn't quite done.

Thank you to Kibibi Devero who was a dedicated editor and copyeditor for the book's text – all my many words would be nothing without the support of her editorial assistance. I want to remember to thank Anu French, a beautiful integrative medicine provider and musician who donated her song "Channel of Shanthi" from her album *Wake Up My Divinity* to the book trailer for this book.

A big hug of thanks to Rev. Dr. Barbara Holmes for writing the foreword to this book. Her work in *Joy, Unspeakable* and the living body of her work and words have meant so much to me in the formation of my authentically POC-centered spirituality, mysticism and personhood. She has also been a great elder in the work of Mystic Soul. I am so grateful for her eldership in this world of POC mysticism where there are few visibilized Christian-oriented living POC mystics and her modeling of her own mystic way in the world has been invaluable to me and many others.

And finally, a thank you to The Mystic Soul Project community which has offered its abundant support of this book and its birth into the world.

ABOUT THE AUTHOR

TERESA MATEUS, LCSW, E-RYT 200, is a trauma psychotherapist, adjunct professor of Social Work, meditation and integreative healing practitioner, author and speaker on spirituality, activism, trauma and healing. She is a co-founder and Executive Director of The Mystic Soul Project – a non-profit centering POC/QTPOC voices at the intersection of mysticism, activism and healing. She is also the co-creator of TRACC4Movements – a training and education program for Trauma Response & Crisis Care for Movements (social movements).

Teresa has a graduate degree in Clinical Social Work from New York University as well as a 200-hour yoga teacher training in the Sivananda tradition. She is also a graduate from the Center for Action and Contemplation's two-year Living School program.

She is the author of a psycho-educational memoir titled *Mending Broken: A Journey Through the Stages of Trauma & Recovery* as well as *Sacred Wounds: A Path to Healing from Spiritual Trauma*.

Teresa currently resides in Chicago, Illinois where she lives in an apartment on the northside of the city which she has titled her "hermitage in the city" and which she shares with her two dogs – Gaia and Faith.

You can learn more about Teresa at www.teresamateus.com.

ABOUT MYSTIC SOUL PRESS

Mystic Soul Press is an initiative of The Mystic Soul Project, a 501c3 nonprofit organization based in Chicago but engaging with POC (people of color) & QTPOC (queer and trans people of color)-centering at the intersections of spirituality, activism and healing throughout the US & the world.

Mystic Soul Press continues and extends the mission of centering POC at the intersection of spirituality, activism and healing by offering a platform to lift up the voices, works and wisdom of POC who often don't have access to or fit the traditional boxes of the mainstream publishing industry.

Mystic Soul Press is committed to engaging exciting frontiers of literary works and offering a space for folks to share their wisdom and have access to the wisdom of other POC & QTPOC folks.

Mystic Soul Press is committed to publishing at least 2-4 new works a year in addition to the annual Mystic Soul Anthology which will be themed in relationship with the Mystic Soul Conference theme for that year.

To learn more please visit www.mysticsoulpress.com.

Made in the USA
Las Vegas, NV
26 March 2023

69723500R00100